Coding with Python

Your Guide to Become a Better Programmer with Advanced Methods and Strategies

Mathias Carlsson

ISBN: 9798640225754

Table of Contents

Introduction

This book will help you learn advanced coding in Python. The first is to install Python. I used Python IDLE which is also called Python shell for encoding. I also used Python text editor to write and run full programs. You can open an editor. First open the shell and then open a new file from the file menu on the top bar. The newly opened file will look different because it is not a shell, but a text editor. Once you have written a program in the editor, you can run it by clicking f5. The editor will ask you to save the file. Save and run it to get the results.

What does this book offer you?

This book is for advanced Python readers. I assume you've already learned how to write a script in Python. The book is divided into several chapters with information on various topics. Let's see what the chapters of the book have for the readers.

- The first chapter introduces you to the basics of Python. The first section of the first chapter will help you learn the procedure for downloading Python. You will learn how to download it on the Windows operating system. Since the Windows operating system is the most widely used of all the operating systems in the world, learn how to search for, install and use Python installation at will. I'll explain how to use the interactive shell in Python; that is what you can see in the list of installed programs. You can open it and write a piece of code to see how it performs. Next, I will explain how to post comments in Python using docstrings. I'll explain how to add a single line and multi-line comments in the code to use them as a reference. Then I move on to Python variables. You learn to name variables according to the tradition of Python. I will shed light on various Python data types such as string, float and integer. You will see their use in the coming chapters when we actually start programming. The chapter ends with an explanation of Python operators. This chapter is good as an overview of the different concepts of Python. Otherwise, it is good for the beginner who is just trying to step into the world of Python.

- The second chapter explains the two main elements of Python: lists and tuples. They are so important in Python that they are part of almost all of the Python programs you are going to write. The first part of the chapter discusses the individual values in a list and how to change these values. I will then explain how to make a loop in a list. The loop loops through all the items in a list and displays them neatly in the Python shell where you can read and use them. The following section explains how to remove items from a list using the pop () method. You can delete the very last item one by one from the list until the list is empty. The next section deals with the concatenation of lists. You can add two or more lists into a combined whole. This helps link small lists that a business agency gets from users and combines them into a gigantic whole. Next comes the role of lists in Python programming. You can use them while developing a game in which a soldier has to carry a wide variety of weapons to fight the enemy. Combined with Python lists are Python tuples, which are used to create immutable lists. They are useful, but are rigid and work well when you cannot allow users to change the contents of a list. Python is quite a flexible language because it even allows tuples to change. There is a special method for doing that, which I explained in the last section of the chapter.

- The next chapter is about dictionaries. In the beginning you will learn how to write a simple dictionary. Next, I will explain how to add different sets of values to a dictionary. You can add as many key pair values as you want after you create and save a dictionary. In the next section I will explain how to make a loop in a dictionary to display all dictionary items in the shell. It is quite useful because it helps you see what you have stored in a dictionary. If you run a financial consultancy, this feature allows you to view heavy sets of dictionaries that have saved your valuable customers' data. Next, I will explain how to remove various items from the dictionary. The next section is about deletion. Although the delete function allows you to delete individual items from the dictionary, the delete option allows you to delete the entire dictionary. Very useful if you permanently close a certain part of your company, but terrible if you accidentally do it. You can also create a list in a dictionary and use it at will. I made a list of weapons that a soldier will carry in a game. The list exists in a dictionary. It saved me a lot of effort that would otherwise have gone into creating different key pair values. I'll explain how to nest a dictionary in another. The last part of the chapter highlights the get () method.

- The next chapter is about Python loops. I will explain the while loop and the for loop in this chapter. The while loop is important because it allows programmers to enter into the programs different conditions that are true or false. In both ways, they help make the program easy to use. I will explain the importance of the break statement and the continuous statement in helping readers create effective programs. The while loop is both interesting and dangerous. You need it if you want to create a game that reaches the logical end if the user wants to leave it. It is the while loop that makes this possible; otherwise the user will see the screen hanging.

- The next chapter is about Python functions. It is a general overview of how functions are created in Python, how to add parameters and print instructions in functions. I'll explain the purpose of Python functions and how to create certain parameters. The importance of positional arguments is also fully explained, and you learn how poorly positioned arguments can destroy a function's execution. I'll explain the default parameters that fill the function call if you leave the parameters blank. I'll tell you how writing the parameters makes a difference when it comes to the position of the parameters and how you can get the parameters to fill in where they are intended.

- The next chapter is about Python classes. This is quite a long chapter and it will teach you how to create objects in Python. Python classes bring this language closer to object-oriented languages such as Javascript. You will learn how to create a class in Python. A lesson can be anything, such as a cat, car, peacock, motorcycle and panda. I created a class called Panda. You will learn how to make a Panda sit, eat, roll, laugh and fight with other pandas. It all happens in Python classes. This is where real programming begins. I'll explain the importance of instances in Python. I will create many instances in the Python class to help you learn how to build a program.

- In the following example, I am going to another class called the Motorbike class. In this lesson I will explain how to build a program that is intended for a motor showroom. You can create different objects for this program. Each object can be based on a certain type of engine. You can add further details of the motorcycle within the major class instances. I explained in detail how to display the information the user needs and how to add certain attributes to the main class of Python. I will add several attributes to Python's main class, such as the mileage functions, to add new mileage to the existing mileage. I will help you write a special program that will prevent your employees from reversing mileage to get more profit from the customer. It is a kind of lock that you can put in your code to make it impossible to change. You can take the code and practice and see the result in the Python shell and match them with the one I wrote in the book. By matching the codes and the results, you will learn the mistakes you make if your codes don't work. The chapter ends with an explanation of importing the class. You cannot write all codes from larger programs in one file. Multiple files are stored on your computer. You can get their name and import them into the program you are creating. I import the parent classes and the child classes I created. All classes refer to engines from the previous examples. It's quite an interesting feature of Python and I promise you will learn the process with pleasure!

- The last chapter of the book shows several Python programs. I tried to create games and simple programs in Python that you can see and learn from. You can also copy the code and paste it into the text editor to see how it works. Once you understand the text of the code, you can easily make custom changes and view the results. You can add more math operators to the Python calculator. You can also make many other changes to make the code custom and interesting. This will help you learn practical skills.

This book is at an advanced level. Therefore I have not explained any strings, etc., nor have I gone into the details of list, tuples and functions. Most of the book is focused on programming. If you are a beginner, focus on the first few sections for an overview of the basics of Python. I have done all the encoding in Python 3.8 and I request that you download and install the same version to avoid frustration. Enjoy your coding experience!

Chapter 1: Introduction to the basics of Python

Python has proven to be a useful language over time. Its use is increasing rapidly. This chapter walks you through the steps involved in downloading and installing Python. You will also learn how to control the shell window and IDLE and what the meaning of each is. In addition, I will also give you a look at the basics of Python.

How to download Python

To learn and use Python, you need access to the Python interpreter. Let's see how to download them.

- The very first way to access Python is to access the Python.org website from Python Software Foundation. You can download the most appropriate installer that suits your computer system and then run it on the system.
- Some of the operating systems such as Linux offer a package manager, which you can run to install Python.
- On Mac systems, you can download and install Python from a package manager called Homebrew.
- You can also install Python as an application on mobile operating systems such as iOS and Android. This is a great option to practice coding skills on the go.

In addition, there are some websites that give users access to a Python interpreter without any installation on the computer.

How to install on Windows

The Windows operating system is unlikely to have been shipped to your door with Python preinstalled. Fortunately, installation includes downloading the Python installer from python.org. After installation, you can run it. Let's see how many steps are involved in installing Python Windows.

- The first step is to open a browser and navigate to the download page on python.org.
- You must go to the version you need to download such a Python 2 or Python 3. Click here.
- Now scroll down to the bottom of the page and then select Windows86 o 64 which suits you best.
- Now you need to run the installer you downloaded. Once you've run it by double-clicking it, you'll see a window with the 'Install now' button in the middle of the box. Check the box titled 'Add Python to Path' at the bottom of the installer. Then click on 'Install now'.
- A few minutes later you will see Python installed on your Windows operating system.

Python programming consists of a wide variety of syntactic constructs and interactive environment functions. Python is one of the few fun sills to add to your skills for making small programs.

How to use the interactive shell

If you go to the Windows menu on your Windows operating system, you can find Python's interactive shell named IDLE that you installed with Python. Open it up. You will see the >>> prompt in your interactive Windows shell. Now let's see how the interactive shell works. I used some math operators in the Python shell to see the results.

```
IDLE 2.6
>>> 4 + 4
8
>>> 4 * 4
16
>>> 4/4
1
>>> 4-4
0
>>>
```

In the above example, I used all four of the basic math operators to see how the shell works. Every time the shell completes a math function, the shell prompt is returned.

The IDLE window should contain some text at the top. It should look like this:

```
Python 2.6 (r26: 66721, October 2, 2008, 11:06:43 AM) [MSC
v.1500 64 bit (AMD64)] on win32
Type "copyright", "credits" or "license ()" for more information.
************************************************* * **
```

Personal firewall software can warn of the IDLE connection makes its subprocess using the internal loopback of this computer

couple. This connection is not visible on any external interface and no data is sent to or received from the internet.

```
************************************************* * **
```

You should ignore the text and start writing your code where the text ends. If you're using a version of Python, the shell may look a little different. Let's see.

```
Python 3.8.1 (tags / v3.8.1: 1b293b6, December 18, 2019,
10:39:24 PM) [MSC v.1916 32 bit (Intel)] on win32
Type "help", "copyright", "credits" or "license ()" for more
information.
>>>
```

It is much shorter and simpler than Python 2.6. The line with code 4 + 4 is mentioned as an expression in Python. An expression is considered the most basic type of programming statement in Python. They can consist of values such as 2, 4, 8 and operators such as +, * and /. So the characters of +, * and - in the code lines are called operators. If you write code that computers don't understand, Python will throw an error. The program may crash due to the error you made while writing the code. If you want to know more about the error and how to fix it, you can copy and google the error code to see how other people have solved it. You can also view Python errors and meanings.

Post comments in Python

Comments in Python can be used to explain the code you wrote and make the code readable. Comments in Python start with #. If you don't put # at the beginning of the comment, ignore it.
>>> # This is an example of a comment in Python
>>> print ("I want to learn Python.")
I want to learn Python.
>>>
You can also put them at the end of the line and this has no effect on the code. Likewise, they can be written in the middle of the code if the code is long. You can also use a comment to prevent Python from executing code. Let's take a look at the following example.
>>> # print ("I want to learn Python.")
>>>

There can be multiple lines in Python for comment. There is no special syntax for multi-line comments. If you want to add a multi-line comment in Python, you can do that by inserting a # before each line of comments. These may seem like three individual comments, but this technique works well if you want to add a long comment on three lines.

```
>>> #This is a note
>>> #that consists of
>>> # three lines.
>>> print ("I want to learn Python.")
I want to learn Python.
>>>
```

There is another way out. You can insert a multi-line string into the code by using triple codes. Place the comment within the triple codes to leave a comment in the code.

Python variables

A variable in Python is similar to a box in a computer's memory, a place where you can store a single value. Once the value is stored in a variable, you can use it later in another calculation. Value is usually stored in a variable using an assignment statement, which consists of the name of the variable, an equal sign called as an operator, and a value. For example, if the assignment state is x = 54, the name of the variable is "x" and the entire value is 54 stored in it. In simple words, you can take a variable as a box labeled with a name, which in this case is "x" and a value that is inside the box.

```
>>> tomato = 5
>>> tomato
5
>>> potato = 10
```

```
>>> potato
10
>>> tomato + potato
15
>>> pepper = 50
>>> pepper
50
>>> tomato + potato + pepper
65
```

We can also change the value of a variable after we create it. It's as easy as adding two variables, as we did in the example above. You know the current value of tomato is 5. I'll add another number to it to check if I can add it or not.

```
>>> tomato = tomato + 10
>>> tomato
15
>>>
```

Rules for naming variables

When it comes to naming the variables, we must adhere to some guidelines and rules. If you break the rules, you will get an error. Variable names can only contain a number, an underscore and a letter. You can start a variable name with a number, but not with a letter or underscore. You may not add spaces in the names of the variables. If you do that, the shell will show errors. You cannot use the names of Python functions and other Python keywords. The variable should not be too long. Keep it short. Also, be careful about using lowercase l and uppercase O as the shell can confuse them with the binary digits I and O.

Python data types

The data type is very important in programming because you can assign different types of data to variables and each data type has a specific use in a given code and calculation. Python also has some built-in data types by default. Let's take a look at some basic data types in Python.

```
>>> x = str ("shotgun, pistol, revolver")
>>> print (x)
shotgun, pistol, revolver
>>> x = int (50)
>>> print (x)
50
>>> x = frozenset (("shotgun", "pistol", "revolver"))
>>> print (x)
frozenset (['shotgun', 'pistol', 'revolver'])
>>> x = float (15.5)
>>> print (x)
15.5
>>> x = dict (gun_name = "shotgun", number_of_guns = "5")
>>> print (x)
{'number_of_guns': '5', 'gun_name': 'shotgun'}
>>> x = range (10)
>>> print (x)
[0, 1, 2, 3, 4, 5, 6, 7, 8, 9]
>>> x = list (("shotgun", "revolver", "pistol"))
>>> print (x)
['shotgun', 'revolver', 'pistol']
>>> x = bytes (5)
>>> print (x)
5
>>> x = tuple (("shotgun", "revolver", "pistol"))
>>> print (x)
```

('shotgun', 'revolver', 'pistol')
>>> x = bool (5)
>>> print (x)
Right
>>> x = complex (5y)
>>> print (x)
5y
>>> x = set (("shotgun", "revolver", "pistol"))
>>> print (x)
set (['shotgun', 'pistol', 'revolver'])
>>>

Each data type has a specific use when it comes to Python encoding. I will use different data types in the codes in the following chapters. The data types I used in the code snippet above are strings, integers, floats, complex, frozen sets, sets, lists, tuples, bytes, range, and dictionaries.

Python operators

Python operators are actually used to perform certain operations on Python variables. There are different types of Python operators, such as mapping operator, logical operator, bitwise operator, identity operator, comparison operator, and membership operator. In the first phase, I will explain what arithmetic operators are and how they are used to perform certain functions.

>>> x = 10
>>> y = 5
>>> #Addition (+)
>>> x + y
15
>>> # Division (/)

```
>>> x / y
2.0
>>> #Floor division (//)
>>> x // 5
2
>>> x // y
2
>>> #Modulus (%)
>>> x% y
0
>>> #Multiplication (*)
>>> x * y
50
>>> #Subtract (-)
>>> x - y
5
>>> #Exponentiation (**)
>>> x ** y
100000
>>>
```

In the above code snippet I first assigned values to two variables and then I started explaining and using the operators on the variables and got different results. Each line of the code has a new arithmetic operator and its application to the variables. These variables can be used in the Python code to get different results. For example, if you develop a game about a hunter who has to kill his enemies to get to the target, where he has to defuse a bomb to save the world. He needs certain weapons along the way. You can use the addition operator when the hunter picks up a gun or snatch one of the other soldiers on the go, and the subtraction operator when he picks up ammunition for a gun or just wants to get rid of it on the go. During practical applications of Python coding, these operators help you add interactivity to the project you are working on. There's no question that users love the interactivity in a game or software program they've used.

Chapter 2: Python Lists and Tuples

Python list is one of the topics you need to understand before writing programs. Python list and python tuples must be read and understood at the same time. Python lists and tuples allow users to pack a wide variety of values, making it easier to write even complex programs that can handle large amounts of data. Because lists can contain other lists, you can use them to organize data in a coherent and hierarchical form. I'll explain the basics of python lists and tuples in this chapter. You will learn how to use lists to manipulate data.

A list is generally a container that can contain a range of values in a coherent and well-ordered order. List value, a term, is a value that can be stored in any variable you have created. I already explained in the previous chapter how to save data in a list. Let's review the information. A list could look like this: [shotgun, revolver, pistol]. String values are typed in quotes to tell the shell where the string starts and where it ends. Likewise, a list starts with a square bracket and ends with a square closing bracket []. All values in the list are dubbed as items. You must separate these items using commas. You can give them a comma-separated name. You must enter the following into the interactive shell.

```
>>> gun_list = ['shotgun', 'pistol', 'revolver']
>>> print (gun_list)
['shotgun', 'pistol', 'revolver']
>>>
```

Obtain individual values with indices

If you have a list like the one I used as an example in the previous section, you can get the values of various items from the list using their index numbers. This is simple and takes little time to complete. The whole number in square brackets used to categorize the list items is known as an index. One of the important things to know about indexes in the list is that the first value in the list is at index 0. The second value is at 1 and so on. For example, we can recall different items from a list using the index number they have. When developing a game in which there is a hunter with guns, you can list all the weapons and allow the user to choose one using the index numbers. It will be quite a hassle if not frustration on the part of the user to manually go through the entire list of weapons to choose. I already referred to the game in the previous section. Without the help of indices, the game will no longer be as fun as it should be.

```
>>> gun_list = ['shotgun', 'pistol', 'revolver', 'rifle']
>>> gun_list [0]
'shotgun'
>>> gun_list [1]
'gun'
>>> gun_list [2]
'revolver'
>>> gun_list [3]
'gun'
>>>
```

A special thing about Python lists is that you can change them, reorder them and include duplicate numbers in them too. As we are trying to understand about indexing, it is relevant to mention here that negative indexing starts at the back. You can recall certain items from the list using negative values.

```
>>> gun_list = ["shotgun", "pistol", "revolver", "rifle"]
```

```
>>> gun_list [-3]
'gun'
>>> gun_list [0]
'shotgun'
>>> gun_list [-2]
'revolver'
>>> gun_list [-1]
'gun'
>>>
```

If you want to give the player more choice in terms of choosing weapons from the storage he has, you can add another list function to the code that controls a player's ammunition. Add the series of indices to the list that allow the player to pick up a certain number of weapons from the list. He can carry more than one gun to fight the enemy. The range of indices function also specifies the starting point of the range and the ending point. I will compile a long list this time and then choose different ranges to display different items.

```
>>> gun_list = ["shotgun", "pistol", "revolver", "rifle", "bazooka",
"handgun", "Ak-47"]
>>> print (gun_list [1: 5])
['pistol', 'revolver', 'rifle', 'bazooka']
>>> print (gun_list [2: 7])
['revolver', 'rifle', 'bazooka', 'handgun', 'Ak-47']
>>> print (gun_list [3: 6])
['rifle', 'bazooka', 'handgun']
>>> print (gun_list [3: 9])
['rifle', 'bazooka', 'handgun', 'Ak-47']
>>>
```

You can see that I have easily recalled different value ranges from the list. In the end, I went out of range of the list, but Python shell redirected me to the last item in the list. This is good if the player chooses the wrong number, he would automatically select the end of the range. It keeps us in the flow of the game.

There are more interesting things you should know about the range in python lists. You have seen that there are generally two values in a Python list, such as an initial value and an end value. You can omit the starting value while writing the range, and it starts from the first item in the list by default.

```
>>> gun_list = ["shotgun", "pistol", "revolver", "rifle", "bazooka", "handgun", "Ak-47"]
>>> print (gun_list [: 5])
['shotgun', 'pistol', 'revolver', 'rifle', 'bazooka']
>>> print (gun_list [: 9])
['shotgun', 'pistol', 'revolver', 'rifle', 'bazooka', 'handgun', 'Ak-47']
>>> print (gun_list [:])
['shotgun', 'pistol', 'revolver', 'rifle', 'bazooka', 'handgun', 'Ak-47']
>>> print (gun_list [2:])
['revolver', 'rifle', 'bazooka', 'handgun', 'Ak-47']
>>> print (gun_list [5:])
['handgun', 'Ak-47']
>>>
```

I experimented with several things in the above code snippet. For example, I left out the first number from the range. I then omitted both numbers from the range and you saw that the shell published the whole list. Then I left out the second number in the range function that worked fine and started printing the items from the index number next to the number I wrote for the colon in the code. The start point is specified while the end is open. If you leave the end value blank, the list will complete.

How to change the value of an item

In your game, you need to add some spice by allowing the player to change the set of weapons you gave him. You may allow him to steal other soldiers' weapons, take them off the street, remove them from dead soldiers, or steal them from the enemy's ammo supplies. To do that interactively and effectively, you need to make your code flexible by allowing the player to update the list of weapons. Python allows you to change the value of an item in the list. I will update the list of weapons by replacing the existing items with new ones.

```
>>> gun_list = ["shotgun", "pistol", "revolver", "rifle", "bazooka", "handgun", "Ak-47"]
>>> gun_list [2] = "grenade"
>>> print (gun_list)
['shotgun', 'pistol', 'grenade', 'rifle', 'bazooka', 'pistol', 'Ak-47']
>>> gun_list [5] = "knife"
>>> print (gun_list)
['shotgun', 'pistol', 'grenade', 'rifle', 'bazooka', 'knife', 'Ak-47']
>>>
```

This code is good for adding some interactivity to your game, but it can't be called the best choice. It is an option and not the ultimate choice because by using this the player can only replace a gun. He will first have to throw a gun or draw bullets from all rounds to make room for the new gun. Only then can he add more weapons.

Create a loop in a list

You can loop through this list by adding the "for" loop. This feature allows the player to display any weapon in his possession. He will be able to see and estimate how much ammunition he has and whether it is enough to fight the enemy or not.

```
>>> gun_list = ["shotgun", "pistol", "revolver", "rifle", "bazooka", "handgun", "Ak-47"]
>>> for x in gun_list:
print (x)

shotgun
pistol
revolver
rifle
bazooka
hand gun
AK-47
>>>
```

You can check whether a particular item is in the list or not by using the 'if' statement. This feature allows you to give your player the freedom to check whether a certain type of weapon is in his backpack or not. This will certainly add to the interactivity of your game and players will feel more free. Let's see how to add this feature to your code. Open the Python IDLE again and create a list first.

```
>>> gun_list = ["shotgun", "pistol", "revolver", "rifle", "bazooka", "handgun", "Ak-47"]
>>> as "gun" in gun_list:
print ("Soldier, 'gun' is available for use.")
Soldier, "gun" is available for use.
>>> as "gun" in gun_list:
```

```
print ("Soldier, 'revolver' is available for use.")
Soldier, 'revolver' is available for use.
>>> as "grenade" in gun_list:
print ("Soldier, 'grenade' is available for use.")
>>> as "shotgun" in gun_list:
print ("Soldier, 'gun' is available for use.")
Soldier, "gun" is available for use.
>>> as "shotgun" in gun_list:
print ("Soldier, 'shotgun' is available for use.")
Soldier, 'shotgun', is available for use.
>>>
```

In the above code snippet, I recalled certain weapons from the list and they were printed. When I tried to print the gun that was not in the gun, I got a blank line back. Also important is the print statement when you are actually developing a game. You must create a different print statement for each item in the list. You can see that I intentionally did not change the print statement and tried to display a particular gun. The scale could not decipher that the gun I wanted to show was of a different type than the gun I included in the print statement. When I corrected the print statement, I was able to display the correct type of gun I remembered. So you need to make a new print statement for each gun when developing a game.

Another important feature of lists is that they can be changed and updated. This means that you can allow your player to add as many items as he wants. For example, he can collect and store ammunition along the way to use it against the enemy. You can build an ammo store in the game and allow the player to break into it with some effort and rob it of weapons and other types of ammunition available. He can add the new weapons to the list one by one. There is a special method in Python to achieve this goal. It is known as the append () method.

```
>>> gun_list = ["shotgun", "pistol", "revolver"]
>>> gun_list.append ("AK-47")
>>> print (gun_list)
['shotgun', 'pistol', 'revolver', 'AK-47']
>>> gun_list.append ("handgun")
>>> print (gun_list)
['shotgun', 'pistol', 'revolver', 'AK-47', 'handgun']
>>> gun_list.append ("grenade")
>>> print (gun_list)
['shotgun', 'pistol', 'revolver', 'AK-47', 'pistol', 'grenade']
>>> gun_list.append ("rifle")
>>> print (gun_list)
['shotgun', 'pistol', 'revolver', 'AK-47', 'pistol', 'grenade', 'rifle']
>>> gun_list.append ("bazooka")
>>> print (gun_list)
['shotgun', 'pistol', 'revolver', 'AK-47', 'pistol', 'grenade', 'rifle',
'bazooka']
>>>
```

You can see that every item I added to the list was displayed every time I printed the list. That way, you can get the player to build a substantial storage of weapons and pistols to use against the enemy.

There is yet another option that you can give to your users. You can allow them to insert an item in a specific place in the list. Although this option is not very common, it can still be used in places. I mean this is really not required in a game. Players don't care at what position they save the new item. During combat, it makes no sense to decide the position of a particular weapon that the player is holding. However, it can be used in other places as needed. The method used to place a newly collected item is known as the insert () method.

```
>>> gun_list = ["shotgun", "pistol", "revolver"]
```

```
>>> gun_list.insert (2, "rifle")
>>> print (gun_list)
['shotgun', 'pistol', 'rifle', 'revolver']
>>> gun_list.insert (3, "handgun")
>>> print (gun_list)
['shotgun', 'pistol', 'rifle', 'pistol', 'revolver']
>>> gun_list.insert (0, "grenade")
>>> print (gun_list)
['grenade', 'shotgun', 'pistol', 'rifle', 'pistol', 'revolver']
>>>
```

An interesting thing to add to your game is to fill it in with another interesting feature. You can allow your player to collect as many weapons along the way as he needs and then allow him to lose them if he feels extra weight. For this purpose you need the remove () method to throw away certain weapons.

```
>>> gun_list = ["shotgun", "pistol", "revolver", "rifle", "bazooka", "handgun", "Ak-47"]
>>> gun_list.remove ("gun")
>>> print (gun_list)
['shotgun', 'revolver', 'rifle', 'bazooka', 'handgun', 'Ak-47']
>>> gun_list.remove ("rifle")
>>> print (gun_list)
['shotgun', 'revolver', 'bazooka', 'handgun', 'Ak-47']
>>> gun_list.remove ("bazooka")
>>> print (gun_list)
['shotgun', 'revolver', 'handgun', 'Ak-47']
>>> gun_list.remove ("Ak-47")
>>> gun_list.remove ("revolver")
>>> gun_list.remove ("shotgun")
>>> print (gun_list)
['hand gun']
>>> gun_list.remove ("handgun")
>>> print (gun_list)
```

[]
>>>
You can see that I have removed items from the list one by one. I added printing instructions after removing specific guns, but discontinued printing instruction for specific guns. This means you can choose to display the list of remaining weapons after each removal. When the player has thrown all the weapons, the list remains empty.

The Pop () method

There is yet another feature of Python worth considering. It allows players to use a gun and automatically get the next one, because the used gun is automatically popped from the list. The pop () method removes the last item in the list.

```
>>> gun_list = ["shotgun", "pistol", "revolver", "rifle", "bazooka", "handgun", "Ak-47"]
>>> gun_list.pop ()
'AK-47'
>>> print (gun_list)
['shotgun', 'pistol', 'revolver', 'rifle', 'bazooka', 'handgun']
>>> gun_list.pop ()
'hand gun'
>>> print (gun_list)
['shotgun', 'pistol', 'revolver', 'rifle', 'bazooka']
>>> gun_list.pop ()
'bazooka'
>>> print (gun_list)
['shotgun', 'pistol', 'revolver', 'rifle']
>>> gun_list.pop ()
'gun'
>>> print (gun_list)
```

```
['shotgun', 'pistol', 'revolver']
>>>
```

The pop method can be used to make a specific item appear in the list instead of extracting the last one.

```
>>> gun_list = ["shotgun", "pistol", "revolver", "rifle", "bazooka", "handgun", "Ak-47"]
>>> gun_list.pop (0)
'shotgun'
>>> print (gun_list)
['pistol', 'revolver', 'rifle', 'bazooka', 'pistol', 'Ak-47']
>>> gun_list.pop (2)
'gun'
>>> print (gun_list)
['pistol', 'revolver', 'bazooka', 'pistol', 'Ak-47']
>>>
```

In addition to the versatility, lists provide the removal method for encoders. You can remove a specific item from the list. Unlike the pop method, the delete method does not allow you to delete the item at the end of the list.

```
>>> gun_list = ["shotgun", "pistol", "revolver", "rifle", "bazooka", "handgun", "Ak-47"]
>>> del gun_list [0]
>>> print (gun_list)
['pistol', 'revolver', 'rifle', 'bazooka', 'pistol', 'Ak-47']
>>> del gun_list [4]
>>> print (gun_list)
['pistol', 'revolver', 'rifle', 'bazooka', 'Ak-47']
>>>
```

This method allows users to delete the entire list as if it never existed.

```
>>> gun_list = ["shotgun", "pistol", "revolver", "rifle", "bazooka", "handgun", "Ak-47"]
>>> print (gun_list)
```

```
['shotgun', 'pistol', 'revolver', 'rifle', 'bazooka', 'handgun', 'Ak-47']
>>> del gun_list
>>> print (gun_list)
Retrace (most recent call last)
File "<pyshell # 71>", line 1, in <module>
print (gun_list)
NameError: name 'gun_list' is not defined
>>>
```

You can see I made a list and printed it in the shell. I then applied the removal method and when I tried to print the list again in the shell I got an error. This means that the list is no longer stored in the shell.

If you want to keep the list and just remove all items from it, you have the clear () method to apply. The list remains with the same name you gave it, but the items in it are removed.

```
>>> gun_list = ["shotgun", "pistol", "revolver", "rifle", "bazooka", "handgun", "Ak-47"]
>>> gun_list.clear ()
>>> print (gun_list)
[]
>>>
```

You can see that the list is empty. You can also make a copy of a specific list. It's a bit tricky because you have to use the built-in list method.

```
>>> gun_list = ["shotgun", "pistol", "revolver", "rifle", "bazooka", "handgun", "Ak-47"]
>>> new_list = gun_list.copy ()
>>> print (new_list)
['shotgun', 'pistol', 'revolver', 'rifle', 'bazooka', 'handgun', 'Ak-47']
>>> print (gun_list)
['shotgun', 'pistol', 'revolver', 'rifle', 'bazooka', 'handgun', 'Ak-47']
>>>
```

We have another method to copy the list into the shell. These techniques are useful if you have to complete the game with more than one player and each player will have the same option regarding the available weapons.

```
>>> gun_list = ["shotgun", "pistol", "revolver", "rifle", "bazooka", "handgun", "Ak-47"]
>>> newlist = list (gun_list)
>>> print (new list)
['shotgun', 'pistol', 'revolver', 'rifle', 'bazooka', 'handgun', 'Ak-47']
>>>
```

List concatenation

Python allows us to combine two different lists and the method is known as list concatenation. The method is very simple because only one operator is required to complete the task.

```
>>> gun_list = ["shotgun", "pistol", "revolver", "rifle", "bazooka", "handgun", "Ak-47"]
>>> ammunition_list = ["grenade", "missile", "missile launcher"]
>>> weapon combination = weapon list + ammunition list
>>> print (weapon_combo)
['shotgun', 'pistol', 'revolver', 'rifle', 'bazooka', 'pistol', 'Ak-47', 'grenade', 'missile', 'rocket launcher']
>>>
```

Concatenation can be really interesting by choosing a different method. You can now combine two lists by adding the items from the second list to the first list one by one.

```
>>> gun_list = ["shotgun", "pistol", "revolver", "rifle", "bazooka", "handgun", "Ak-47"]
>>> ammunition_list = ["grenade", "missile", "missile launcher"]
>>> for x in ammunition_list:
gun_list.append (x)
```

```
>>> print (gun_list)
['shotgun', 'pistol', 'revolver', 'rifle', 'bazooka', 'pistol', 'Ak-47',
'grenade', 'missile', 'rocket launcher']
>>>
```

Another method of combining two lists is the expand () method, which adds certain elements from one list to the second. This method adds the second list to the end of the first list.

```
>>> gun_list = ["shotgun", "pistol", "revolver", "rifle", "bazooka",
"handgun", "Ak-47"]
>>> ammunition_list = ["grenade", "missile", "missile launcher"]
>>> gun_list.extend (ammunition_list)
>>> print (gun_list)
['shotgun', 'pistol', 'revolver', 'rifle', 'bazooka', 'pistol', 'Ak-47',
'grenade', 'missile', 'rocket launcher']
>>>
```

What makes the expand () method different from the rest of the concatenation methods is the fact that no new list is created by combining two old ones. Instead, the items are retrieved from the second list and added to the first list. Another example makes it easier to understand this.

```
>>> gun_list = ["shotgun", "pistol", "revolver", "rifle", "bazooka",
"handgun", "Ak-47"]
>>> ammunition_list = ["grenade", "missile", "missile launcher"]
>>> ammunition_list.extend (gun_list)
>>> print (ammunition_list)
['grenade', 'missile', 'rocket launcher', 'shotgun', 'pistol',
'revolver', 'rifle', 'bazooka', 'pistol', 'Ak-47']
>>>
```

You can see it depends on the position of the list names in this method. In this example, I took the contents of the first list and added them to the second list. It worked just right.

There is a specific method to compile a list from scratch. You just need to insert the items you want to add to the list and apply the method in the Python shell.

```
>>> gun_list = list (("shotgun", "pistol", "revolver", "rifle",
"bazooka", "handgun", "Ak-47"))
>>> print (gun_list)
['shotgun', 'pistol', 'revolver', 'rifle', 'bazooka', 'handgun', 'Ak-47']
>>>
```

Programming lists

When writing programs, it can be very tempting to create different types of variables to store different values. If you want to store different types of weapons in different variables, you may want to write the code as under:

```
>>> gunType1 = 'shotgun'
>>> gunType2 = 'gun'
>>> gunType3 = 'revolver'
>>> gunType4 = 'AK-47'
>>> gunType5 = 'bazooka'
>>> gunType6 = 'gun'
>>> gunType7 = 'gun'
```

This style of code writing doesn't look right. If you have to change the number of weapons a player can use, you will run into problems. Your program no longer accepts gun names. You can use a single variable that has a list value. Let's create a program that allows a game player to create a list of weapons to use on the field.

To do that you need to start a new Python file and save it with the extension (.py) like python.py. You can open this file from the file menu of IDLE or Python shell. Then open it and write the program. When you have finished writing the program, you can run it by clicking the 'Run' button visible in the top menu. You can also run by pressing the f5 key.

```
gunType = []
while true:
print ('You can enter the name of the gun you want to record' +
str (len (gunType) + 1) +
(Or don't enter anything to stop.):)
gunName = input ()
if gunName == '':
break
gunType = gunType + [gunName] # This code represents
concatenation
print ('The names of the weapons are:')
for gunName in gunType:
print ('' + gunName)
```

This is the program I wrote that allows the player to add items to the list. When a player has added all the items, he can display them by pressing "enter" without writing anything in the program prompt.

============== RESTART: C: / Users / saifia-computers / Desktop / Python.py ==============

You can enter the name of the gun you want to shoot 1 (or enter nothing to stop):

rifle

You can enter the name of the weapon you want to include 2 (or enter nothing to stop):

AK-47

You can enter the name of the weapon you want to include 3 (or enter nothing to stop):

Bazooka
You can enter the name of the weapon you want to include 4 (or enter nothing to stop):
hand gun
You can enter the name of the weapon you want to include 5 (or enter nothing to stop):
shotgun
You can enter the name of the weapon you want to add 6 (or enter nothing to stop):
revolver
You can enter the name of the weapon you want to include 7 (or enter nothing to stop.):
pistol
You can enter the name of the gun you want to shoot 8 (or enter nothing to stop.):
The names of the weapons are:
rifle
AK-47
Bazooka
hand gun
shotgun
revolver
pistol
>>>

This code snippet begins with the text Restart. This indicates that the program is active. Every time you restart a new program, you will see this restart bar.

Lists are considered useful data types in Python because they allow programmers to write code that can work on a modifiable number of values that exist in a single variable. You have learned that you can change the contents of a list by adding, removing or replacing values.

Python Tuples

The Python-tuple data type is so much similar to Python lists that many people wonder what the difference is. They are identical, but there are differences that distinguish them. The very first difference is writing these data types. Python tuples are usually written in parentheses () rather than in square brackets. The following example shows how to write them.

```
>>> gun_types = ('shotgun', 'pistol', 'revolver', 'rifle', 'bazooka', 'handgun')
>>> gun_types [0]
'shotgun'
>>> gun_types [2: 5]
('revolver', 'rifle', 'bazooka')
>>> len (gun_types)
6
>>>
```

Tuples are different because they are immutable. You cannot add, remove or add to tuples any item. You can confirm this by trying to change the value of tuples.

```
>>> gun_types = ('shotgun', 'pistol', 'revolver', 'rifle', 'bazooka', 'handgun')
>>> gun_types [2] = 'missile'
Retrace (most recent call last)
File "<pyshell # 135>", line 1, in <module>
gun_types [2] = 'missile'
TypeError: 'tuple' object does not support item mapping
>>>
```

How to change the values in Python Tuples

Once you have made a tuple, there is no chance that you can change the values in a normal way. Tuples are unchanging, but there is certainly a solution. You can convert tuples in the form of a list, then change the list and then convert the list back into Python tuple. That's why the only one is to convert tuple to a list and then change the values.

```
>>> gun_types = ('shotgun', 'pistol', 'revolver', 'rifle', 'bazooka', 'handgun')
>>> x = list (gun_types)
>>> x [3] = "missiles"
>>> gun_types = tuple (x)
>>> print (gun_types)
('shotgun', 'pistol', 'revolver', 'missiles', 'bazooka', 'handgun')
>>>
```

Like the lists, Python provides the loop function for tuples. You can cycle through tuple items and view the result. The "for" loop will cycle through all tuple items and print the values.

```
>>> gun_types = ('shotgun', 'pistol', 'revolver', 'rifle', 'bazooka', 'handgun')
>>> for y in gun_types:
print (y)

shotgun
pistol
revolver
rifle
bazooka
hand gun
>>>
```

Python makes it possible to check whether a certain item exists in a tuple or not.

>>> gun_types = ('shotgun', 'pistol', 'revolver', 'rifle', 'bazooka', 'handgun')
>>> as "handgun" in gun_types:
print ("Yes, 'handgun' exists in this tuple")
Yes, "gun" exists in this tuple
>>>
When I type the name of the item that does not exist in the tuple, nothing is returned.
gun_types = ('shotgun', 'pistol', 'revolver', 'rifle', 'bazooka', 'handgun')
>>> as "missile" in gun_types:

Chapter 3 : Python dictionaries

In this chapter you will learn more about using dictionaries in your codes. Python dictionaries allow you to connect different pieces of information so that you can use them in a coherent form in your programs. I will explain how to access different pieces of information from a dictionary and how to change a particular piece of information. You learn about the gigantic capacity of dictionaries in terms of information. I explain how to make a loop in a dictionary. You will also learn how to integrate dictionaries into lists.

Dictionaries are important in that they allow programmers to create interactive models of some real-life objects and make them work perfectly. You can create a new dictionary that represents a person and also save the amount of information you want to take with you. For example, when you develop a game, you have to create certain characters in the game. For a character, you have to define his name, age, profession, location and many other aspects such as height, etc.

A simple dictionary

In fact, a dictionary is a collection that is unordered, indexed, and changeable. Python dictionaries are usually written in curly braces. You can add keys and values to the dictionaries after you successfully create them.

```
game_player = {'name': 'delta', 'height': 5, 'lives': 3}
print (game_player ['name'])
print (game_player ['height'])
= RESTART: C: / Users / saifia-computers / Desktop / Python.py
=
```

delta
5
>>>
You can see that the dictionary I created can save the name, height and lives of the game player that I will add to my game. When you run the program, you can print the information you have saved in the dictionary. Dictionary requires a lot of practice before you can perfect it. Once you've mastered the art of dictionary making, you'll see how effectively you can model some real-world situations.

A dictionary in Python is usually a collection of key-value pairs in which each key has a certain value. You can use the key to get the value it is associated with. The value of the key can be a string, number, list, or other dictionary. You have the freedom when it comes to entering the keys with values. You can use an object that you create in Python. You have to wrap your dictionary with curly braces or braces. As you have seen in the example, you have to write a dictionary in the form of pairs. The pair normally contains two values that are linked together. Each key is separated from its value by a colon. The simplest of all dictionaries can have one pair of values.

How to access values in a dictionary

Python dictionaries, like lists, allow programmers access to the value at any point in the code. You must write the name of your dictionary, put the key in square brackets, and then access the item.
```
>>> game_player = {'name': 'delta', 'height': 5, 'lives': 3}
>>> print (game_player ['height'])
5
>>> print (game_player ['name'])
```

delta
>>> print (game_player ['lives'])
3
>>>
You can see that with each keyword, the shell prints the value associated with the key.

Add new values to the dictionary

Python dictionaries are somewhat dynamic structures that allow you to add new key / value pairs to your dictionary at any time. If you want new additions to your existing dictionary, you can add a key / value pair by specifying the name of the dictionary that would be followed by the new key within the square brackets, accompanied by the new values.

In the following code snippet, I will add new pieces of information to my existing dictionary. I will add the details of the ammunition that the player will carry in the game to fight the enemy.

```
>>> game_player = {'name': 'delta', 'height': 5, 'lives': 3}
>>> print (game_player)
{'name': 'delta', 'height': 5, 'lives': 3}
>>> game_player ['gun1'] = 'handgun'
>>> game_player ['gun2'] = 'shotgun'
>>> game_player ['gun3'] = 'revolver'
>>> game_player ['gun4'] = 'rifle'
>>> game_player ['gun5'] = 'gun'
>>> print (game_player)
{'name': 'delta', 'height': 5, 'lives': 3,' gun1 ':' handgun ',' gun2 ':'
shotgun ',' g
un3 ':' revolver ',' gun4 ':' rifle ',' gun5 ':' pistol '}
>>>
```

In the above code snippet, I added five types of weapons that the player will carry when going on a mission. You can see how easy it is to add new key pair values to an existing dictionary. You can add as many items in the dictionary as you want. For example, in the game I'm developing I can add a water bottle, a knife, a card, a bulletproof jacket that the player would use on the way to the enemy's camps.

You can add the key pairs like I did. Once done, you can print the dictionary to check whether or not the new pairs have been added to the dictionary. The latest in the game_player dictionary contains all the key pair values that have been added recently. This technique allows you to create a blank dictionary at the beginning and add values along the way while you are in the development phase of the game.

Sometimes it is quite convenient and even necessary to start a dictionary and add items to it along the way. The first step in this regard is to define a dictionary and then add items to it. Start with an empty set of brackets and then fill it in with key-value pairs. Consider the following example.

```
>>> game_player = {}
>>> print (game_player)
{}
>>> game_player ['name'] = 'delta'
>>> print (game_player)
{'name': 'delta'}
>>> game_player ['height'] = 5
>>> print (game_player)
{'name': 'delta', 'height': 5}
>>> game_player ['lives'] = 3
>>> print (game_player)
{'name': 'delta', 'height': 5, 'lives': 3}
>>> game_player ['gun1'] = 'handgun'
>>> print (game_player)
```

```
{'name': 'delta', 'height': 5, 'lives': 3, 'gun1': 'handgun'}
>>> game_player ['gun2'] = 'shotgun'
>>> print (game_player)
{'name': 'delta', 'height': 5, 'lives': 3, 'gun1': 'handgun', 'gun2':
'shotgun'}
>>> game_player ['gun3'] = 'revolver'
>>> print (game_player)
{'name': 'delta', 'height': 5, 'lives': 3, 'gun1': 'handgun', 'gun2':
'shotgun', 'gun3': 'revolver'}
>>>
```

You can see how each key / value pair is added to the dictionary. Blank dictionaries can be used when you store data provided by the users. You do not have the data in storage. It comes along the way when a user leaves it with you. That's where empty dictionaries come in handy.

You can change values in a dictionary

Python dictionaries allow you to change the values of the key pair. You must enter the name of a dictionary, along with the keys in square brackets. After that you have to fill it in with the new values you want to associate with the specific key.

```
>>> game_player = {'name': 'delta', 'height': 5, 'lives': 3, 'gun1':
'handgun', 'gun2': 'shotgun', 'gun3': 'revolver', 'gun4': 'rifle',
'gun5': 'pistol'}
>>> game_player ['name'] = 'delta2'
>>> print ("The new name of the player is" + game_player
['name'] + ".")
The new name of the player is delta2.
>>> game_player ['gun5'] = 'machine gun'
>>> print ("The player replaced the gun with" + game_player
['gun5'] + ".")
```

The player replaced the gun with a machine gun.
>>>
I defined the name of the dictionary and then I changed the values of the key pair. An interactive game requires that the player has the freedom to do many things. By customizing a dictionary, you can have that freedom.

Loop the dictionary

The Python shell allows you to browse a dictionary using the "for" loop. When you loop through the dictionary, the return values are known as the keys of the dictionary.

```
>>> game_player = {'name': 'delta', 'height': 5, 'lives': 3, 'gun1': 'handgun', 'gun2': 'shotgun', 'gun3': 'revolver', 'gun4': 'rifle', 'gun5': 'pistol'}
>>> for y in game_player:
print (y)

name
height
lives
gun 1
gun2
gun3
gun4
gun5
>>>
```

In the above, I made a loop through the keys of each pair of the dictionary. In the following code snippet, I loop through the values of the dictionary.

```
>>> game_player = {'name': 'delta', 'height': 5, 'lives': 3, 'gun1':
'handgun', 'gun2': 'shotgun', 'gun3': 'revolver', 'gun4': 'rifle',
'gun5': 'pistol'}
>>> for y in game_player:
print (game_player [y])
delta
5
3
hand gun
shotgun
revolver
rifle
pistol
>>>
```

To display the values of each pair of the dictionary, we also have a special function.

```
>>> game_player = {'name': 'delta', 'height': 5, 'lives': 3, 'gun1':
'handgun', 'gun2': 'shotgun', 'gun3': 'revolver', 'gun4': 'rifle',
'gun5': 'pistol'}
>>> for y in game_player.values ():
print (y)
delta
5
3
hand gun
shotgun
revolver
rifle
pistol
>>>
```

If you want to add an interesting feature to your game that will allow your player to view the general specification of a particular character of the game, you will definitely enjoy using the items () feature. This function allows you to display both the keys and the values of a particular dictionary.

```
>>> game_player = {'name': 'delta', 'height': 5, 'lives': 3, 'gun1':
'handgun', 'gun2': 'shotgun', 'gun3': 'revolver', 'gun4': 'rifle',
'gun5': 'pistol'}
>>> for y, z in game_player.items ():
print (y, z)
name delta
height 5
lives 3
gun1 pistol
gun2 shotgun
gun3 revolver
gun4 rifle
gun5 pistol
>>>
```

You can see that we have displayed perfect pairs of the dictionary neatly in the shell. There is a specific keyword in Python that allows users to find out whether or not a particular key is in the dictionary. This feature is relatively useful in banks and financial consultancies where programmers have to search through a lot of data to find the information they need. The "in" keyword helps them know whether or not a particular key is in the dictionary.

```
>>> game_player = {'name': 'delta', 'height': 5, 'lives': 3, 'gun1':
'handgun', 'gun2': 'shotgun', 'gun3': 'revolver', 'gun4': 'rifle',
'gun5': 'pistol'}
>>> as "gun3" in game_player:
print ("Yes, 'gun3' is one of the keys in the game_player's
dictionary.")
```

Yes, 'gun3' is one of the keys in the game_player dictionary.

If you want to check the total length of the dictionary, you can do it with the following method.

```
>>> game_player = {'name': 'delta', 'height': 5, 'lives': 3, 'gun1': 'handgun', 'gun2': 'shotgun', 'gun3': 'revolver', 'gun4': 'rifle', 'gun5': 'pistol'}
>>> print (len (game_player))
8
>>>
```

How to remove items from a dictionary

Like lists, you can also remove items from dictionaries. In the following code snippet, I will apply the method to the dictionary I built for you. This method is useful when you are developing a program and you want to remove certain key-value pairs.

```
>>> game_player = {'name': 'delta', 'height': 5, 'lives': 3, 'gun1': 'handgun', 'gun2': 'shotgun', 'gun3': 'revolver', 'gun4': 'rifle', 'gun5': 'pistol'}
>>> game_player.pop ('name')
'delta'
>>> print (game_player)
{'height': 5, 'lives': 3,' gun1 ':' handgun ',' gun2 ':' shotgun ',' gun3 ':' revolver ',' gun4 ':' rifle ',' gun5 ':' gun '}
>>> game_player.pop ('alive')
3
>>> print (game_player)
{'height': 5, 'gun1': 'handgun', 'gun2': 'shotgun', 'gun3': 'revolver', 'gun4': 'rifle', 'gun5': 'pistol'}
>>> game_player.pop ('gun1')
'hand gun'
>>> print (game_player)
```

{'height': 5, 'gun2': 'shotgun', 'gun3': 'revolver', 'gun4': 'rifle',
'gun5': 'pistol'}
>>> game_player.pop ('gun3')
'revolver'
>>> print (game_player)
{'height': 5, 'gun2': 'shotgun', 'gun4': 'rifle', 'gun5': 'pistol'}
>>>

If you're wondering if you can remove the last item from a dictionary, just like you did in the lists, you can do that with the method popitem (). The popitem () method is useful in that you don't have to name the key to delete it. But I have to say that this method is only useful for a general dictionary narrowing. It is too arbitrary to be used for deleting items from a dictionary.
>>> game_player = {'name': 'delta', 'height': 5, 'lives': 3, 'gun1': 'handgun', 'gun2': 'shotgun', 'gun3': 'revolver', 'gun4': 'rifle', 'gun5': 'pistol'}
>>> game_player.popitem ()
('gun5', 'gun')
>>> print (game_player)
{'name': 'delta', 'height': 5, 'lives': 3,' gun1 ':' handgun ',' gun2 ':' shotgun ',' gun3 ':' revolver ',' gun4 ':' gun '}
>>> game_player.popitem ()
('gun4', 'rifle')
>>> print (game_player)
{'name': 'delta', 'height': 5, 'lives': 3, 'gun1': 'handgun', 'gun2': 'shotgun', 'gun3': 'revolver'}
>>> game_player.popitem ()
('gun3', 'revolver')
>>> print (game_player)
{'name': 'delta', 'height': 5, 'lives': 3, 'gun1': 'handgun', 'gun2': 'shotgun'}
>>> game_player.popitem ()
('gun2', 'shotgun')

```
>>> print (game_player)
{'name': 'delta', 'height': 5, 'lives': 3, 'gun1': 'handgun'}
>>>
```

The del keyword

Python has the del keyword for deleting certain items after you specify the names of the keys. This prevents you from randomly pulling out items from your dictionary. You can take a targeted approach to remove items you don't want in the dictionary.

```
>>> game_player = {'name': 'delta', 'height': 5, 'lives': 3, 'gun1':
'handgun', 'gun2': 'shotgun', 'gun3': 'revolver', 'gun4': 'rifle',
'gun5': 'pistol'}
>>> del game_player ['name']
>>> print (game_player)
{'height': 5, 'lives': 3,' gun1 ':' handgun ',' gun2 ':' shotgun ',' gun3
':' revolver ',' gun4 ':' rifle ',' gun5 ':' gun '}
>>> del game_player ['gun3']
>>> print (game_player)
{'height': 5, 'lives': 3, 'gun1': 'handgun', 'gun2': 'shotgun', 'gun4':
'rifle', 'gun5': 'pistol'}
>>>
```

Warning! Use the del keyword carefully as it can delete the whole dictionary in one go. Let's demonstrate.

```
>>> game_player = {'name': 'delta', 'height': 5, 'lives': 3, 'gun1':
'handgun', 'gun2': 'shotgun', 'gun3': 'revolver', 'gun4': 'rifle',
'gun5': 'pistol'}
>>> del game_player
>>> print (game_player)
Retrace (most recent call last)
File "<pyshell # 96>", line 1, in <module>
print (game_player)
```

NameError: name 'game_player' is not defined

>>>

You can see that the Python shell returned an error, meaning it cannot recognize the name of the dictionary because it has already removed it. There is another clear () keyword that can be used to empty the dictionary. The difference between deleting and emptying is that deletion stops the dictionary as you can see in the last code snippet, but the clear () keyword only empties the dictionary, meaning the dictionary remains.

>>> game_player = {'name': 'delta', 'height': 5, 'lives': 3, 'gun1': 'handgun', 'gun2': 'shotgun', 'gun3': 'revolver', 'gun4': 'rifle', 'gun5': 'pistol'}
>>> game_player.clear ()
>>> print (game_player)
{}
>>>

There is a special method that allows you to copy the dictionary. Copying a dictionary is not easy. We must apply a method to achieve this goal. Python has a built-in method for making copies of dictionaries.

>>> game_player = {'name': 'delta', 'height': 5, 'lives': 3, 'gun1': 'handgun', 'gun2': 'shotgun', 'gun3': 'revolver', 'gun4': 'rifle', 'gun5': 'pistol'}
>>> game_player2 = game_player.copy ()
>>> print (game_player2)
{'name': 'delta', 'height': 5, 'lives': 3,' gun1 ':' handgun ',' gun2 ':' shotgun ',' gun3 ':' revolver ',' gun4 ':' rifle ',' gun5 ':' pistol '}
>>>

You can see we have an exact copy of the game_player dictionary. This is useful if you are building a financial consultancy program where you risk losing important data to hackers or other types of security breaches. You can use the copy () method to make exact copies of the dictionaries that contain data that you have collected from your customers or visitors to your website. With a few copies, you can save all the data in case you lose the original dictionary. Interestingly, this copy is one hundred percent similar to the original dictionary. There is no difference between the two in quality and use. It means that you can apply all code to a copy just like the original.

Python has another built-in method to copy a dictionary. It is known as the dict () method. This adds to the variety that Python gives to programmers.

```
>>> game_player = {'name': 'delta', 'height': 5, 'lives': 3, 'gun1': 'handgun', 'gun2': 'shotgun', 'gun3': 'revolver', 'gun4': 'rifle', 'gun5': 'pistol'}
>>> game_player2 = dict (game_player)
>>> print (game_player2)
{'name': 'delta', 'height': 5, 'lives': 3,' gun1 ':' handgun ',' gun2 ':' shotgun ',' gun3 ':' revolver ',' gun4 ':' rifle ',' gun5 ':' pistol '}
>>>
```

Like the others, the dict () method also helps us make a perfect copy of our dictionary.

A list in a dictionary

Python allows you to create a list of dictionaries. Sometimes it is not possible to create a general dictionary that contains all the important information about a certain character of a game. For example, you can create different dictionaries for the name and height of your game's character because they fall into a physical category. You can create a separate dictionary for the lives it has and another dictionary for the weapons it carries. Then you can put them all in one list. Let's demonstrate this.

```
>>> game_player = {'name': 'delta', 'height': 5}
>>> game_player1 = {'lives': 3}
>>> game_player2 = {'gun1': 'handgun', 'gun2': 'shotgun', 'gun3': 'revolver', 'gun4': 'rifle', 'gun5': 'pistol'}
>>> game_playerG = [game_player, game_player1, game_player2]
>>> for game_player in game_playerG:
print (game_player)
{'name': 'delta', 'height': 5}
{'alive': 3}
{'gun1': 'handgun', 'gun2': 'shotgun', 'gun3': 'revolver', 'gun4': 'rifle', 'gun5': 'pistol'}
>>>
```

At first I created three separate dictionaries and then put all three into a single dictionary called game_playerG. Each of the three dictionaries represents some of the features of the game's character. I then looped through the list of dictionaries and displayed the items of all three dictionaries.

Nest a list in a dictionary

Instead of listing the dictionaries, you can create a list in a dictionary. It is quite useful to put a list in a dictionary. For example, we can make a list of weapons in a dictionary to further simplify it. Or if you work in a restaurant for which you develop a program that contains all the ingredients of a certain dish. You can add certain ingredients in the form of a list in a dictionary. This will help you simplify storage. In the following example, I will explain how to make a list in a dictionary to make it more readable and smoother.

```
>>> game_player = {'name': 'delta', 'height': 5, 'lives': 3, 'guns':
['handgun', 'shotgun', 'revolver', 'rifle', 'pistol' ],}
>>> for weapons in game_player ['weapons]:

SyntaxError: EOL when scanning literal strings
>>> for weapons in game_player ['weapons']:
print ("\ t" + guns)
hand gun
shotgun
revolver
rifle
pistol
>>>
```

I made a list in a dictionary in the code snippet above. This is a way to simplify the process. I also made a mistake in the code. You can see I forgot a comma in the code which resulted in an error. You have to watch out for these kinds of errors to make the code easy and error free.

```
>>> fav_language = {
'ben': ['french', 'english'],
'norah': ['spanish'],
'john': ['english', 'french'],
```

'tibay': ['chinese', 'spanish'],
}
>>> for name, languages in fav_language.items ():
print ("\ n" + name.title () + "s favorite languages are:")
for language in languages:
print ("\ t" + language.title ())
Ben's favorite languages are:
French
English
The most popular languages of Norah are:
Spanish
John's favorite languages are:
English
French
Tibay's top fav languages are:
Chinese
Spanish
>>>

In the above code snippet, I made a list in a dictionary to show the best way to do that. You can create multiple lists within a dictionary if you add multiple objects within one dictionary. Since I had to cram multiple objects into a single dictionary, I had to create several lists of the characteristics of all those objects that I had to include (Matthes, 2016).

Dictionaries are usually not ordered. You can enter them with random values for the keys that allow you to organize the data in different ways. I'm going to create a program where you can save a user's name and the language he or she knows. You can use names like keys and languages as values in the program. You will need to open a new editor window and save the file with the extension .py.

The dictionary I am going to create contains user names and the languages they know. You can use the key to check for a name in the dictionary by using a keyword. You can keep adding new names to the program and the languages they know, and the program will update the database in seconds.

```
fav_language = {
'ben': 'french',
'norah': 'spanish',
'john': 'english',
'tibay': 'chinese',
}
while true:
print ('Enter a name: (blank to exit)')
name = input ()
as name == '':
break
as name in fav_talen:
print (name + 'knows' + fav_talen [name])
different:
print ('There is no information about the languages' + name +
'knows')
print ("What languages does he or she know?")
flang = input ()
fav_language [name] = flang
print ('language database updated')
======= RESTART: C: / Users / saifia-computers / Desktop / Python.py ======
Enter a name: (empty to stop)
am
am know french
Enter a name: (empty to stop)
norah
norah knows spanish
```

Enter a name: (empty to stop)
John
john knows english
Enter a name: (empty to stop)
tibay
Tibet knows Chinese
Enter a name: (empty to stop)
carmen
There is no information about the languages that Carmen knows
Which languages does he or she know?
Italian
language database updated
Enter a name: (empty to stop)
carmen
carmen knows italian
Enter a name: (empty to stop)
johnson
There is no information about the languages that Johnson knows
Which languages does he or she know?
Hungarian
language database updated
Enter a name: (empty to stop)
johnson
Johnson knows Hungarian
Enter a name: (empty to stop)
Sylvia
There is no information about the languages Sylvia knows
Which languages does he or she know?
Latin
language database updated
Enter a name: (empty to stop)
Sylvia
Sylvia knows Latin

Enter a name: (empty to stop)
The point where the RESTARTS code is when the program starts running the shell. You can continue to add new names and languages to complete the program. (Sweigart, 2015)

Get () method

Long dictionaries make it difficult to locate certain keys and their values. Fortunately, there is a special get () method you can use to figure out information you want to see in a dictionary. I am testing the get () method in the Python shell.

```
>>> game_player = {'name': 'delta', 'height': 5, 'lives': 3, 'guns':
['handgun', 'shotgun', 'revolver', 'rifle', 'pistol' ],}
>>> print (game_player.get ("gun5"))
No
>>> print (game_player.get (weapons))
Retrace (most recent call last)
File "<pyshell # 133>", line 1, in <module>
print (game_player.get (weapons))
NameError: name 'weapons' is not defined
>>> print (game_player.get ("guns"))
['handgun', 'shotgun', 'revolver', 'rifle', 'pistol']
>>> print (game_player.get ("name"))
delta
>>>
```

On the first attempt, the shell did not recognize the key; therefore it has not returned anything. In the second, I missed the commas, so the shell returned an error. On the third attempt, I successfully displayed the values of the key. Since it had more than one value, it returned the same. In fact, a list was displayed by the Python shell when I tried to find out the values of the main 'weapons'.

Chapter 4 : Python Loop

Python programming, like all other types of coding, is intended to solve the problems that end users face. To do that, you need to get additional information from the end user. For example, if someone needs to check if he is eligible to play on the basketball team or if he is qualified to vote in the elections, you can create a program that can give him the correct answer he needs.

In this type of program, we need to know the age of the user before we give an answer, which means that we have to build an interface that asks for an answer from the user regarding his or his age. The user will enter his or her age into the program using the input () method. Once he or she reaches age, they can know the answer. You can design your program to ask them their name so you can save their information for future reference. This chapter explains the importance of the input () method and the while loop so that you can use them in your programs to make them more effective.

The input () method

The input () method is actually a stop for Python programs because it waits for the user to fill in the program with some text. Once the Python program has received the user's input, it can store the same in some kind of variable that you create yourself. This makes programming and operation easy. I have created a program that repeats the information you enter in the shell prompt. It is interesting. Let's check it out.

```
message = input ("This program repeats everything you write. Just like a parrot:")
print (message)
```

= RESTART: C: / Users / saifia-computers / Desktop / Python.py
This program repeats everything you write. Like a parrot:
Terminator has been destroyed.
Terminator has been destroyed.
>>> John
Retrace (most recent call last)
File "<pyshell # 136>", line 1, in <module>
John
NameError: name 'John' is not defined
>>>
= RESTART: C: / Users / saifia-computers / Desktop / Python.py
>>>
This program repeats everything you write. Just like a parrot: I
have been selected for the basketball team.
I have been selected on the basketball team.
>>>
You can see that the program returns whatever you say to it. The
second attempt gave an error because I did not run the program
again. This means that you have to run the program from the
beginning every time you want to run it.
The program took an argument from the user. It was a kind of
instruction that the adhering program used exactly the same
wording as the user entered. The prompt asks users to enter the
information they want to display in the shell. When the user
presses enter, he executes the instructions.
You should write a clean code to make it easier for users to
understand and act on the instructions. The prompt should be
clear and easy to follow so that the user knows what to do. Let's
write another program with the input () method.
qualification = input ("Enter your name and educational
qualification:")
print ("Your information:" + qualification + "!")
= RESTART: C: / Users / saifia-computers / Desktop / Python.py

Enter your name and teaching qualification: John, MA (English literature)
Your data: John, MA (English literature)!
>>>
If you want to write a longer code that spans multiple lines, you can do that with the input () function in Python. For example, if you want to let the user know why you need a certain type of information, you can add an extra line in the code. This code is longer than one line. This is useful because users cannot easily enter the program with their personal information if you do not tell them why you need a piece of information in the first place. To achieve this goal, you can add the prompt within a variable and then pass the variable to the input () function.

```
prompt = "We need your information to provide you with a custom job search."
prompt + = "\ nEnter your name and educational qualification:"
qualification = input (prompt)
print ("Your information:" + qualification + "!")
= RESTART: C: / Users / saifia-computers / Desktop / Python.py
```

We need your data to let you search for a tailor-made job.
Enter your name and teaching qualification: Mazhar, MSc (Computer Science)
Your data: Mazhar, MSc (Computer Science)!
>>>
Let's dig deeper into how the input () function works. When entering information in the input () function, Python interprets it as a string. Let's see how to enter numeric numbers. For example, you require the age of the user to put in the record so you can do that with the following method.

```
user_age = input ("what is your legal age?")
= RESTART: C: / Users / saifia-computers / Desktop / Python.py
```

>>>
what is your legal age? 23

```
>>> user_age
'23'
>>>
= RESTART: C: / Users / saifia-computers / Desktop / Python.py
what is your legal age? 54
>>> user_age
'54'
>>>
```

The user's age information has been successfully stored in the variable called user_age. When we ask Python to return the number, it returns in quotes, meaning it is interpreted as a string. If you want to use the same as a number, an error is displayed.

```
= RESTART: C: / Users / saifia-computers / Desktop / Python.py
what is your legal age? 25
>>> user_age> = 25
Retrace (most recent call last)
File "<pyshell # 143>", line 1, in <module>
user_age> = 25
TypeError: '> =' not supported between instances of 'str' and 'int'
>>>
```

Python displays an error because it cannot compare a string to an integer. This problem can be solved if you use the int () function in your code. It teaches Python how to treat an input as a numeric value. It converts a string representation of a given number into a numeric representation. You can tell Python to interpret a number as it is and to perform the math function you want. You can run a conditional test by Python to see if your age is greater than or equal to 25 or not.

```
user_age = input ("what is your legal age?")
user_age = int (user_age)
if user_age> = 25:
```

print ("\ nYou are legally entitled to vote!")
different:
print ("\ nYou are not eligible to vote. Return to your home.")
= RESTART: C: / Users / saifia-computers / Desktop / Python.py
what is your legal age? 20
You are not eligible to vote. Please go back to your house.
>>>
= RESTART: C: / Users / saifia-computers / Desktop / Python.py
>>>
what is your legal age? 25
You are legally eligible to vote!
>>>
= RESTART: C: / Users / saifia-computers / Desktop / Python.py
what is your legal age? 24
You are not eligible to vote. Please go back to your house.
>>>
= RESTART: C: / Users / saifia-computers / Desktop / Python.py
what is your legal age? 30
You are legally eligible to vote!
>>>
You can see in the examples above that Python is fully competent in recognizing the numbers. It calculated perfectly and answered my questions when I entered different numbers in the program.

The While Loop

A while loop can be used to count numbers and perform various other tasks efficiently.

my_num = 1
while my_num <= 10:
print (my_num)

```
my_num + = 1
```

```
= RESTART: C: / Users / saifia-computers / Desktop / Python.py
1
2
3
4
5
6
7
8
9
10
>>>
```

The while loop requires that all variables in the code remain ready. The Python while loop has a break statement that helps us stop the statement at whatever point we want the loop to stop. We need to add the true element which means that the loop will continue as long as the condition is true.

```
a = 1
while a <10:
print (a)
if a == 5:
break
a + = 1
```

```
= RESTART: C: / Users / saifia-computers / Desktop / Python.py
1
2
3
4
5
>>>
```

While loop is very interesting. I'll write the program that repeated what I said to it and then put it in the while loop. The while loop will keep the program running unless you press the keyword that I will put in the program. Let's see.

```
prompt = "\ nMy creator made me repeat what you say:"
prompt + = "\ nI will continue unless you enter 'stop' to terminate the program."
a = ""
while a! = 'stop':
a = input (prompt)
print (a)
= RESTART: C: / Users / saifia-computers / Desktop / Python.py
My creator made sure to repeat everything you say:
I will continue unless you enter 'stop' to terminate the program.
I feel dizzy.
I feel dizzy.
My creator made sure to repeat everything you say:
I will continue unless you enter 'stop' to terminate the program.
Are you dizzy
Are you dizzy
My creator made sure to repeat everything you say:
I will continue unless you enter 'stop' to terminate the program.
How did you learn Python?
How did you learn Python?
My creator made sure to repeat everything you say:
I will continue unless you enter 'stop' to terminate the program.
You repeat so well.
You repeat so well.
My creator made sure to repeat everything you say:
I will continue unless you enter 'stop' to terminate the program.
You are like a parrot.
You are like a parrot.
My creator made sure to repeat everything you say:
```

I will continue unless you enter 'stop' to terminate the program.
stop
stop
>>> Can you repeat it now?
SyntaxError: invalid syntax
>>>
You can see that after I quit, the program no longer accepts and repeats my text. This way you can get rid of the while loop. If the thought goes around in your mind that or you can use a different value instead of quitting, I'll make it easier for you to understand the following example. I will use the same program, but a different value to end the program.
prompt = "\ nMy creator made me repeat what you say:"
prompt + = "\ nI will continue unless you enter 'stop it' to terminate the program:"
a = ""
while a! = 'stop it':
a = input (prompt)
print (a)

= RESTART: C: / Users / saifia-computers / Desktop / Python.py
My creator made sure to repeat everything you say:
I will continue unless you enter 'quit' to end the program: I want to reach the top of Mount Everest.
I want to reach the top of Mount Everest.
My creator made sure to repeat everything you say:
I will continue unless you enter 'quit' to end the program: quit it
stop
>>>

The prompt in a while loop defines what action a user should take. It tells him that there are generally two options: write what he or she wants to repeat or exit the program. Python ran the while loop and repeated multiple statements that I entered into the program. When I wanted to end the program, I managed to do it by entering the keyword I set to separate from the while loop.

There is still a problem. Python takes the keyword, stop it, as a message. It ends the loop, but also displays the same text. The rest of the code is retained, but there will be a small change to note.

```
prompt = "\ nMy creator made me repeat what you say:"
prompt + = "\ nI will continue unless you enter 'stop it' to
terminate the program:"
a = ""
while a! = 'stop it':
a = input (prompt)
if a! = 'stop it':
print (a)
= RESTART: C: / Users / saifia-computers / Desktop / Python.py
My creator made sure to repeat everything you say:
I will continue unless you enter 'quit' to end the program: I want
to reach the top of Mount Everest.
I want to reach the top of Mount Everest.
My creator made sure to repeat everything you say:
I will continue unless you enter 'quit' to end the program: quit it
>>>
```

(Matthes, 2016)

This kind of program interruption may not work properly when developing complex programs such as a game. Different types of events can end the game such as the end of life, the end of ammunition and something else like this. This requires that your program does not end until multiple conditions are met. We can use a flag in complex programs. The program can run as long as the flag is set to true and it will stop when one of the events in the game sets the flag value to false.

```
prompt = "\ nMy creator made me repeat what you say:"
prompt + = "\ nI will continue unless you enter 'stop it' to
terminate the program:"
a = True
while a:
msg = input (prompt)
if msg == 'stop it':
a = not true
different:
print (msg)
= RESTART: C: / Users / saifia-computers / Desktop / Python.py
My creator made sure to repeat everything you say:
I will continue unless you enter 'quit' to end the program: quit it
>>>
```

The program starts in an active state and runs the program as long as it remains true. When a user enters "quit", the program terminates because the condition is set to false. The loop is executed unless it is set to false.

The Break Statement

You can exit the loop at any time using the break statement. To terminate the while loop abruptly, you can enter the break statement. When developing a game, you must enter the break statement so that users can break the while loop to end the game. If you do not include the break statement in your code, the user will not be able to stop the game. This can cause the computer to hang, forcing the user to restart the machine to get out and break the loop. Let's create a program where the player is in a supermarket and buys household items for his home. He can buy endless things. When he is in the game, you must stop at the maximum number of groceries he or she can buy. You can allow her to end the loop using the break statement. As soon as the break statement is applied, the while loop stops immediately.

```
prompt = "\ nEnter the name of the vegetable you want to add to your cart:"
prompt + = "\ n (Enter 'finish' to finish shopping:"
while true:
veg = input (prompt)
if veg == 'finish':
break
different:
print ("I'd like to buy" + veg.title () + "!")
= RESTART: C: / Users / saifia-computers / Desktop / Python.py
Enter the name of the vegetable you want to add to your cart:
(Enter 'finish' to finish shopping: potato
I want to buy Potato!
Enter the name of the vegetable you want to add to your cart:
(Enter 'finish' to finish shopping: tomato
I would like to buy Tomato!
Enter the name of the vegetable you want to add to your cart:
(Enter 'finish' to finish shopping: garlic
```

I want to buy garlic!
Enter the name of the vegetable you want to add to your cart:
(Enter 'finish' to finish shopping: ginger
I want to buy Ginger!
Enter the name of the vegetable you want to add to your cart:
(Enter 'finish' to finish shopping: spinach
I want to buy Spinach!
Enter the name of the vegetable you want to add to your cart:
(Enter 'finish' to finish shopping: finish
>>>

You can see that the loop started as soon as the player entered the vegetable he wanted to buy. It went on and took five vegetables as input. It would continue if I had not broken the loop with 'finish'.

In combination with the break statement is the continuous statement. Instead of breaking the loop without executing the rest of the code, continuously apply the statement to go back to the beginning of the loop. In addition, you must ensure that you do not make endless loops. Each loop needs a way to end running so it won't end forever. Let's see that a single slip of a loop can make an infinite loop.

```
y = 1
while y <= 10:
print (y)
y + = 1
= RESTART: C: / Users / saifia-computers / Desktop / Python.py
1
2
3
4
5
6
7
```

8
9
10
>>>
This statement can be easily converted to an infinite loop if you omit one line of code.
y = 1
while y <= 10:
print (y)

The loop does not stop unless you quit the program by closing it. Try it. The best way to stop committing this error again and again is to go through your while loops to make sure you don't make any mistakes in the code.
total_players = ['delta', 'delta1', 'delta2', 'delta3']
alive_players = []
while total_players:
existing_player = total_players.pop ()
print ("Players fighting:" + existing_player.title ())
alive_players.append (existing_player)
print ("\ nThe following players live after the fight:")
for alive_player in alive_players:
print (alive_player.title ())

============== RESTART: C: / Users / saifia-computers / Desktop / Python.py ==============
Players who fight: Delta3
The following players live after the fight:
Delta3
Players who fight: Delta2
The following players live after the fight:
Delta3
Delta2

Players who fight: Delta1
The following players live after the fight:
Delta3
Delta2
Delta 1
Players who fight: Delta
The following players live after the fight:
Delta3
Delta2
Delta 1
Delta
>>>
(Matthes, 2016)
Another function of Python is to remove values from the list via while loop. You do not need to remove individual items from lists. It is done automatically.

```
vegetables = ['potato', 'tomato', 'potato', 'ginger', 'potato', 'spinach', 'potato', 'garlic']
print (vegetables)
while 'potato' in vegetables:
vegetables. remove ('potato')
print (vegetables)
============= RESTART: C: / Users / saifia-computers / Desktop / Python.py =============
['potato', 'tomato', 'potato', 'ginger', 'potato', 'spinach', 'potato', 'garlic']
['tomato', 'ginger', 'spinach', 'garlic']
>>>
```

The for Loop

The while loop will continue as long as the condition you entered in it is true, but if you want to run a block of code a certain number of times you can use the for loop. Link it to the range () function and you're ready to run it as many times as you need.
print ('I wear')
for i within range (10):
print ('shotgun (' + str (i) + ')')
============== RESTART: C: / Users / saifia-computers / Desktop / Python.py ==============
I carry
shotgun (0)
shotgun (1)
shotgun (2)
shotgun (3)
shotgun (4)
shotgun (5)
shotgun (6)
shotgun (7)
shotgun (8)
shotgun (9)
>>>
A for loop is a type of iteration for a code block over a string that is either a list, a dictionary, a tuple, or a string. Don't confuse it with the keyword for in other programming languages. Instead, it works more like an iterator method found in a number of object-oriented programming languages. The for loop helps us execute some instructions.
vegetables = ['potato', 'tomato', 'ginger', 'garlic', 'spinach']
for y in vegetables:
print (y)

```
============== RESTART: C: / Users / saifia-computers /
Desktop / Python.py ==============
potato
tomato
ginger
garlic
Spinach
>>>
```

This is one of the simplest constructions. I made a 'for' loop in a list. Now I continue to make a loop for a string.

```
>>> for y in "I'm creating a program in Python":
print (y)
I

a
m

c
r
e
a
t
I
n
g

a

p
r
o
g
r
```

a

m

I

n

P

y

t

h

O

n

>>>

The "for" loop, like the while loop, has a break statement that helps the programmer to stop the loop before it reaches the logical end. It means it can be stopped before it cycles through all the items in the list.

```
>>> vegetables = ['potato', 'tomato', 'ginger', 'garlic', 'spinach']
>>> for y in vegetables:
print (y)
if y == "garlic":
break
potato
tomato
ginger
garlic
>>> for y in vegetables:
print (y)
if y == "tomato":
break
potato
tomato
>>>
```

You can see the for loop breaks as I ordered it. You can add another code line to display the list after breaking it.

```
>>> vegetables = ['potato', 'tomato', 'ginger', 'garlic', 'spinach']
>>> for y in vegetables:
if y == "garlic":
break
print (y)
potato
tomato
ginger
>>> for y in vegetables:
if y == "ginger":
break
print (y)
potato
tomato
>>>
```

Where we have the break statement, we also have the continuous statement. The continuous statement helps us stop the iteration of a specific loop and then move on to the next.

```
>>> vegetables = ['potato', 'tomato', 'ginger', 'garlic', 'spinach']
>>> for y in vegetables:
if y == "garlic":
continue
print (y)
potato
tomato
ginger
Spinach
>>> for y in vegetables:
if y == "tomato":
break
print (y)
```

```
potato
>>> for y in vegetables:
if y == "tomato":
continue
print (y)
potato
ginger
garlic
Spinach
>>>
```

In the above code snippet, I added a running statement, then an interrupt statement, then another running statement to give you an idea of how the system works. You can see that the continuous instruction continues the loop after it has stopped briefly at the point where you want it to stop.

In the following code snippet, I will add an else statement in the loop. The else keyword in the for loop specifies a particular code block to run when the loop reaches the end.

Chapter 5 : Python functions

A function is generally a block of code that is only executed if the programmer calls it over time. You can pass certain amounts of data known as parameters to a function. A function can therefore return data. You can create a function by defining it in the Python shell. Let's define our function.

```
>>> def this_funct ():
print ("Hi, I'm creating a function.")
>>> this_function
<function this_function at 0x0400E418>
>>> this_funct ()
Hi, I am creating a function.
>>>
```

When you call a particular function, Python must match each argument within the function with a parameter within the function definition. You must match the values of the function known as positional arguments. To see how they work.

```
>>> def description_animal (animal type, animal name):
"" "This will display useful information about an animal." ""
print ("\ nI have a" + animal type + "in my house.")
print ("My" + animal type + "'s name is" + animal name.title () + ".")
>>> description_animal ()
Retrace (most recent call last)
File "<pyshell # 23>", linc 1, in <module>
description_animal ()
TypeError: description_animal () missing 2 required positional
arguments: 'animal_type' and 'animal_name'
>>> description_animal ('Panda', 'Tom')
I have a Panda at my house.
```

My Panda's name is Tom.

>>>

You can see that each function requires two positional arguments. If you have not filled in the function with the arguments, it returns an error, which you can see in the code snippet. A major advantage of features is that you can make as many calls as you want to include in the code.

```
>>> def description_animal (animal type, animal name):
"" "This will display useful information about an animal." ""
print ("\ nI have a" + animal type + "in my house.")
print ("My" + animal type + "'s name is" + animal name.title () +
".")
>>> description_animal ('Panda', 'Tom')
I have a Panda at my house.
My Panda's name is Tom.
>>> description_animal ('Tiger', 'Willy')
I have a tiger in my house.
My tiger is called Willy.
>>> description_animal ('Lion', 'Harry')
I have a lion in my house.
My lion is called Harry.
>>>
```

An important note to keep in mind is that Python functions are order sensitive. You should keep in mind the original order of the arguments. Changing the order causes deviations in the code. The program is still running, but the order of the positional arguments will change significantly.

```
def description_animal (animal type, animal name):
"" "This will display useful information about an animal." ""
print ("\ nI have a" + animal type + "in my house.")
print ("My" + animal type + "'s name is" + animal name.title () +
".")
description_animal ('Panda', 'Tom')
```

```
description_animal ('Willy', 'Tiger')
description_animal ('Harry', 'Lion')
== RESTART: C: \ Users \ saifia computers \ Desktop \
Python.py ==
I have a Panda at my house.
My Panda's name is Tom.
I have a Willy in my house.
My Willy is called Tiger.
I have a Harry in my house.
My Harry's name is Lion.
>>>
```

But there is a way out. You can enter the keywords if you want the arguments to be correct in the code.

```
def description_animal (animal type, animal name):
"" "This will display useful information about an animal." ""
print ("\ nI have a" + animal type + "in my house.")
print ("My" + animal type + "'s name is" + animal name.title () +
".")
description_animal (animal_type = 'Panda', animal_name =
'Tom')
description_animal (animal_name = 'Willy', animal_type =
'Tiger')
description_animal (animal_name = 'Harry', animal_type =
'Lion')
== RESTART: C: \ Users \ saifia computers \ Desktop \
Python.py ==
I have a Panda at my house.
My Panda's name is Tom.
I have a tiger in my house.
My tiger is called Willy.
I have a lion in my house.
My lion is called Harry.
>>>
```

With Python you can also fill in the function with default values, so that when you leave the parameters open, the function takes the values from the default settings.

```
def description_animal (animal_type = 'Panda', animal_name =
'Tom'):
"" "This will display useful information about an animal." ""
print ("\ nI have a" + animal type + "in my house.")
print ("My" + animal type + "'s name is" + animal name.title () +
".")
description_animal (animal_name = 'Willy', animal_type =
'Tiger')
description_animal (animal_name = 'Harry', animal_type =
'Lion')
description_animal ()
== RESTART: C: \ Users \ saifia computers \ Desktop \
Python.py ==
I have a tiger in my house.
My tiger is called Willy.
I have a lion in my house.
My lion is called Harry.
I have a Panda at my house.
My Panda's name is Tom.
>>>
```

You can see that when I left the brackets empty it took values from the default settings. This makes it easy to use functions.

Chapter 6 : Python classes

Object-oriented programming is what makes Python different from other languages. It's a useful and effective approach to writing clean code and useful software that can be used for everyday activities like calculating things or converting kilometers into kilometers. Object-oriented programming requires you to create classes that represent a number of real-world situations and things. You can create objects based on these classes. When you write classes, you must define how a category of objects should behave. What are the characteristics and how can you use them in life?

When you create a class, you must equip the object with all the attributes that the object would generally have. You can also give it some unique features that you desire. You will be more than surprised to see how Python allows you to model some real world situations using object oriented programming.

You can create an object based on real life. This process is known in the Python world as instantiation. There will be more than one instance in Python to work with. In this chapter I will explain how to write classes in Python and how to create different instances in one class.

Object-oriented programming helps programmers to view the world from a different angle. The animation starts here. You can instruct an object to animate as you want. You know your code, what it can do and how you can eventually manipulate it. Classes make complex challenges easier and smoother for you. The code looks logical and makes sense to you. Your programs will make more sense when you add lessons to it.

How do you make a class?

Anything you can think of can be modeled after Python classes. We can start by writing a simple lesson that is a panda. You can also make a model on any other animal. The first is to collect information about pet pandas. What they do, what they look like and what are their common properties. We call pandas and they also have a certain age and name. The most common with pandas is that they tend to roll and sit to eat bamboo. This is information we have about them. You can visit a zoo or watch a YouTube documentary about pandas to see how they behave naturally. You can then model your class based on that information. At this point, I will add the name and age of the panda in the classroom and then I will add two natural behaviors of the panda in the classroom. The two natural behaviors are to eat bamboo and to roll to play and digest the food. The class I'm going to create will tell Python to create an object that would represent a real panda. There will be individual instances in the class that I would use to animate the object.

The Panda class

The next class consists of pandas. In the cases I am going to create in the panda class, the name and age of the object I am going to create will be saved. The panda is given the freedom to sit to feed itself with bamboo and then roll on the ground to digest the food and play with other pandas or to entertain the children watching the object on their screens.

class Panda ():

"" "This is an attempt to create a class that models a panda." ""

def __init __ (self, name, age):

```
        "" "This initializes my class name and age attributes." ""
        self.name = name
        self.age = age


    def sits (itself):
        "" "This simulates sitting a panda when you are in command." ""
        print (self.name.title () + "is currently eating bamboo.")
    def roll_over (itself):
        "" "This will simulate the panda rolling when you give the
        command." ""
        print (self.name.title () + "rolls on the ground!")
```

This is an example of the panda class I wrote in the text editor. You can see many things you may not understand. I will explain each line of code in detail in the following sections of this chapter. In the first line of code I defined the class and named it as Panda. Capitalized names generally refer to classes in Python. That is a tradition that you should keep in mind and follow. The brackets within the definition of the class are empty and the reason for this is that we create a new class from the beginning. There is no additional information about the objects that already exist. I also added docstring in class to explain the details about each line of code.

The init () function you saw in the code above can be called a method because it is part of a class. It works just like a function, but the name changes when it is inside a class. The _init_ () method is a kind of special method that Python automatically executes when a new instance is created based on the Panda class. This method is structured so that there are two underscores and also a few underscores behind. This is also a tradition in Python that helps prevent Python's default method names from conflicting with the names of the methods you create.

The _init _ method I created has three parameters: self, age and name. The self parameter is needed to define the method. It must also precede the rest of the parameters. There are two variables at the end. The name variable stores the name of the object, while the age variable stores the age of the object. The first is in the data type string, while the second is in the numeric data type. The dog class also has two other methods: sit () and roll_over () that animate the object in question. These methods do not require additional information. These methods cause the panda to sit and roll to make it more realistic. You can write this class for an animated object or for a robot. It will act according to the instructions you will fill it with.

Class instances

Now it's time to create instances within Python. An instance is a set of instructions for the class to respond to. Here we can create examples that represent the pandas we need to create.

```
class Panda ():
"" "This is an attempt to create a class that models a panda." ""

def _init _ (self, name, age):
"" "This initializes my class name and age attributes." ""
self.name = name
self.age = age

def sits (itself):
"" "This simulates sitting a panda when you are in command." ""
print (self.name.title () + "is currently eating bamboo.")
def roll_over (itself):
"" "This will simulate the panda rolling when you give the
command." ""
```

```
print (self.name.title () + "rolls on the ground!")

my_panda = Panda ('Tom', 10)
print ("My panda's name is" + my_panda.name.title () + ".")
print ("My panda is" + str (my_panda.age) + "years old.")
============== RESTART: C: \ Users \ saifia computers \
Desktop \ Python.py ==============
My panda's name is Tom.
My panda is 10 years old.
>>>
```

I created an instance in class using the previous class example. I actually told Python to create a panda whose name I wrote as Tom and whose age I defined as 10. Python shell reads the line and calls the _init_ method I put in the Panda class. I also added the arguments Tom and 10 in the Panda class to instruct Python what the instance actually contains. The Python automatically returns an instance representing a panda. I had to create a new variable name as my_panda which stored the information about the new instance. There is yet another naming convention. You can see that I assigned upper case letters to the name of the class which is Panda and smaller letters to the my_panda instance. This naming convention is also useful because we can easily distinguish between the major class and instances while writing a longer code.

Once an instance is created, we can call any method that exists in the Python class. The following Python methods cause the panda to sit and eat bamboo and roll on the floor.

```
class Panda ():
"" "This is an attempt to create a class that models a panda." ""

def _init _ (self, name, age):
"" "This initializes my class name and age attributes." ""
self.name = name
```

```python
    self.age = age

    def sits (itself):
    "" "This simulates sitting a panda when you are in command." ""
    print (self.name.title () + "is currently eating bamboo.")
    def roll_over (itself):
    "" "This will simulate the panda rolling when you give the
    command." ""
    print (self.name.title () + "rolls on the ground!")


my_panda = Panda ('Tom', 10)
print ("My panda's name is" + my_panda.name.title () + ".")
print ("My panda is" + str (my_panda.age) + "years old.")
my_panda.sit ()
my_panda.roll_over ()
============= RESTART: C: \ Users \ saifia computers \
Desktop \ Python.py =============
My panda's name is Tom.
My panda is 10 years old.
Tom is currently sitting to eat bamboo.
Tom rolls on the floor!
```

I gave the name of the instance, which in this case is my_panda. I called the methods and let the panda do what I wanted. Python reads the methods and acts according to the instructions to give a neat representation in the shell. Let's complicate the lesson by adding some additional methods that could help you create more interactive programs. I'll make Panda smile and climb the tree by adding methods.

```python
class Panda ():
    "" "This is an attempt to create a class that models a panda." ""


    def __init __ (self, name, age):
    "" "This initializes my class name and age attributes." ""
```

```python
        self.name = name
        self.age = age

    def sits (itself):
        "" "This simulates sitting a panda when you are in command." ""
        print (self.name.title () + "is currently eating bamboo.")
    def roll_over (itself):
        "" "This will simulate the panda rolling when you give the
command." ""
        print (self.name.title () + "rolls on the ground!")
    def smile (yourself):
        "" "This will simulate the panda 's smile when you give the
command." ""
        print (self.name.title () + "laughs!")
    def climb_up (itself):
        "" "This will simulate the panda climbing up when you command
it." ""
        print (self.name.title () + "climbs up the tree!")
    def battle (itself):
        "" "This will simulate the panda fight when you are in
command." ""
        print (self.name.title () + "fight other pandas.")

my_panda = Panda ('Tom', 10)
print ("My panda's name is" + my_panda.name.title () + ".")
print ("My panda is" + str (my_panda.age) + "years old.")
my_panda.sit ()
my_panda.roll_over ()
my_panda.smile ()
my_panda.climb_up ()
my_panda.fight ()
============== RESTART: C: \ Users \ saifia computers \
Desktop \ Python.py ==============
```

My panda's name is Tom.
My panda is 10 years old.
Tom is currently sitting to eat bamboo.
Tom rolls on the floor!
Tom laughs!
Tom climbs the tree!
Tom fights with other pandas.
>>>
You can also add more instances and methods to the panda class
to make it more interactive and easy to use. At the moment we
only use one copy for the panda class. In the following code
snippet, I will add two more instances to make it even more
complicated. Python reads through every instance and applies all
the methods we've created so far.

```python
class Panda ():
"" "This is an attempt to create a class that models a panda." ""

def _init _ (self, name, age):
"" "This initializes my class name and age attributes." ""
self.name = name
self.age = age

def sits (itself):
"" "This simulates sitting a panda when you are in command." ""
print (self.name.title () + "is currently eating bamboo.")
def roll_over (itself):
"" "This will simulate the panda rolling when you give the
command." ""
print (self.name.title () + "rolls on the ground!")
def smile (yourself):
"" "This will simulate the panda 's smile when you give the
command." ""
print (self.name.title () + "laughs!")
```

```python
def climb_up (itself):
"" "This will simulate the panda climbing up when you command
it." ""
print (self.name.title () + "climbs up the tree!")
def battle (itself):
"" "This will simulate the panda fight when you are in
command." ""
print (self.name.title () + "fight other pandas.")


my_panda = Panda ('Tom', 10)
print ("My panda's name is" + my_panda.name.title () + ".")
print ("My panda is" + str (my_panda.age) + "years old.")
my_panda.sit ()
my_panda.roll_over ()
my_panda.smile ()
my_panda.climb_up ()
my_panda.fight ()
this_panda = Panda ('Harry', 7)
print ("My panda's name is" + this_panda.name.title () + ".")
print ("My panda is" + str (this_panda.age) + "years old.")
this_panda.sit ()
this_panda.roll_over ()
this_panda.smile ()
this_panda.climb_up ()
this_panda.fight ()
that_panda = Panda ('Willy', 12)
print ("My panda's name is" + that_panda.name.title () + ".")
print ("My panda is" + str (that_panda.age) + "years old.")
that_panda.sit ()
that_panda.roll_over ()
that_panda.smile ()
that_panda.climb_up ()
that_panda.fight ()
```

============== RESTART: C: \ Users \ saifia computers \ Desktop \ Python.py ==============
My panda's name is Tom.
My panda is 10 years old.
Tom is currently sitting to eat bamboo.
Tom rolls on the floor!
Tom laughs!
Tom climbs the tree!
Tom fights with other pandas.
My panda's name is Harry.
My panda is 7 years old.
Harry is currently eating bamboo.
Harry rolls on the floor!
Harry laughs!
Harry climbs the tree!
Harry fights with other pandas.
My panda's name is Willy.
My panda is 12 years old.
Willy is currently eating bamboo.
Willy rolls to the ground!
Willy smiles!
Willy climbs the tree!
Willy fights with other pandas.
>>>

I successfully made three pandas called Tom, Harry and Willy.
All three pandas are instructed to do the same. Python reads the instance and makes the pandas do the same thing over and over.

How can classes be used?

Classes can be used to represent a different real-world situation. Once you write them, spend the rest of the time creating and polishing the instances in your class. One of the first things to do is to change the attributes associated with a specific instance. These attributes can be changed later. I will create a class for a bookstore like below:

```
class BookShop:
numberOfBooks = 0

def _init _ (self, title, author, year):
self.title = title
self.author = author
self.year = year
BookShop.numberOfBooks + = 1

def booksInfo (itself):
print ("Book title:", self.title)
print ("Author name:", self.author)
print ("The year of publication:", self.year, "\ n")
# I will create a virtual bookstore here
b1 = BookShop ("Bleak House", "Charles Dickens", 1799)
b2 = BookShop ("War and Peace", "Leo Tolstoy", 1699)
b3 = BookShop ("Dr. Faustus", "Christopher Marlow", 1565)
b4 = BookShop ("The Alchemist", "Paulo Cohelo", 1999)
# You must call member functions for each object
b1.booksInfo ()
b2.booksInfo ()
b3.booksInfo ()
b4.booksInfo ()
print ("BookShop.numberOfBooks:", BookShop.numberOfBooks)
```

============= RESTART: C: \ Users \ saifia computers \ Desktop \ Python.py =============
The title of the book: Bleak House
Author's name: Charles Dickens
The year of publication: 1799
The title of the book: War and Peace
The author's name: Leo Tolstoy
The year of publication: 1699
The title of the book: Dr. Faustus
Author's Name: Christopher Marlow
The year of publication: 1565
The title of the book: The Alchemist
Author's name: Paulo Cohelo
The year of publication: 1999
BookShop.numberOfBooks: 4
>>>

This type of python class is very useful when it comes to real-life situations. You can use this program for your bookstore. You can keep adding new books as instances and it will keep adding it to the total number of books you can see at the end of the code.

```python
class BookShop:
numberOfBooks = 0

def __init__ (self, title, author, year):
self.title = title
self.author = author
self.year = year
BookShop.numberOfBooks + = 1

def booksInfo (itself):
print ("Book title:", self.title)
print ("Author name:", self.author)
print ("The year of publication:", self.year, "\ n")
```

```
# I will create a virtual bookstore here
b1 = BookShop ("Bleak House", "Charles Dickens", 1799)
b2 = BookShop ("War and Peace", "Leo Tolstoy", 1699)
b3 = BookShop ("Dr. Faustus", "Christopher Marlow", 1565)
b4 = BookShop ("The Alchemist", "Paulo Cohelo", 1999)
b5 = BookShop ("Mid March", "George Eliot", 1789)
b6 = BookShop ("Othello", "William Shakespeare", 1589)
# You must call member functions for each object
b1.booksInfo ()
b2.booksInfo ()
b3.booksInfo ()
b4.booksInfo ()
print ("BookShop.numberOfBooks:", BookShop.numberOfBooks)
============== RESTART: C: \ Users \ saifia computers \
Desktop \ Python.py ==============
The title of the book: Bleak House
Author's name: Charles Dickens
The year of publication: 1799
The title of the book: War and Peace
The author's name: Leo Tolstoy
The year of publication: 1699
The title of the book: Dr. Faustus
Author's Name: Christopher Marlow
The year of publication: 1565
The title of the book: The Alchemist
Author's name: Paulo Cohelo
The year of publication: 1999
BookShop.numberOfBooks: 6
>>>
```

You can see that the more books I add to the class, the better it gets and the total number of books is shown at the ends of the shell. (Agarwal, n.d.)

Create the engine class

It's time to create the Motorbike class that stores information about the bikes that will be shown in your showroom. There will be a method in the class that will contain all the information in it.

Class Motor ():

"" "This is a simple attempt to make a motorcycle." ""

def _init _ (self, company, model, year):

"" "Initializes a set of attributes to describe a car." ""

self.company = company

self.model = model

self.year = year

def get_descriptive_name (itself):

Return a neatly formatted descriptive name. ""

long_name = str (self.year) + '' + self.company + '' + self.model

return long_name.title ()

my_bike = Motorcycle ('BMW', 'B7', 2012)

print (my_bike.get_descriptive_name ())

I defined the Motorbike class at the beginning and then I added the _init _ () method which included the self parameter. Consult the Panda class to invoke the self parameter. We need to include three different parameters for this, such as company, model, year. The _init _ () method retrieves all parameters and stores them all within the attributes then associated with the instances created from the class. To create a new class instance, you must specify the engine company name, model, and year to complete the necessary information.

In the next step, I will add an extra attribute to the Python class that will change over time as it will calculate the engine mileage over a given time lapse. The attribute called odometer_reading starts with the value 0 and then continues. There is another method called read_odometer that needs to be added along with the attribute. The method helps us to understand and read the odometer of the car.

```
Class Motor ():
"" "This is a simple attempt to make a motorcycle." ""
def _init _ (self, company, model, year):
"" "Initializes a set of attributes to describe a car." ""
self.company = company
self.model = model
self.year = year
self.odometer_reading = 0

def get_descriptive_name (itself):
Return a neatly formatted descriptive name. ""
long_name = str (self.year) + " + self.company + " + self.model
return long_name.title ()
def read_odometer (itself):
"" "This method prints a specific statement that shows the
mileage of the car." ""
print ("This Motorbike has run" + str (self.odometer_reading) +
"miles.")
my_bike = Motorcycle ('BMW', 'B7', 2012)
print (my_bike.get_descriptive_name ())
my_bike.read_odometer ()
============== RESTART: C: \ Users \ saifia computers \
Desktop \ Python.py =============
Bmw B7 from 2012
This motorcycle has run 0 miles.
>>>
```

Python calls the __init__ () method to create a new instance and it also stores the company name, model of the bike and year of its brand as attributes. Then there is a new feature that calculates the miles a motorcycle has traveled. I also added a new method called read_odometer (). This makes the process easier to calculate the mileage of the engine. Python automatically counts the mileage every time the engine is running.

```
Class Motor ():
"" "This is a simple attempt to make a motorcycle." ""
def __init__ (self, company, model, year):
"" "Initializes a set of attributes to describe a car." ""
self.company = company
self.model = model
self.year = year
self.odometer_reading = 5


def get_descriptive_name (itself):
Return a neatly formatted descriptive name. ""
long_name = str (self.year) + '' + self.company + '' + self.model
return long_name.title ()
def read_odometer (itself):
"" "This method prints a specific statement that shows the mileage of the car." ""
print ("This Motorbike has run" + str (self.odometer_reading) + "miles.")
my_bike = Motorcycle ('BMW', 'B7', 2012)
print (my_bike.get_descriptive_name ())
my_bike.read_odometer ()
============== RESTART: C: \ Users \ saifia computers \ Desktop \ Python.py =============
Bmw B7 from 2012
This motorcycle has run 5 miles.
```

>>>

You can see that I added 5 miles in the odometer feature. The rest of the code remains the same. We can add more miles.

```
Class Motor ():
"" "This is a simple attempt to make a motorcycle." ""
def _init _ (self, company, model, year):
"" "Initializes a set of attributes to describe a car." ""
self.company = company
self.model = model
self.year = year
self.odometer_reading = 0
def get_descriptive_name (itself):
Return a neatly formatted descriptive name. ""
long_name = str (self.year) + '' + self.company + '' + self.model
return long_name.title ()
def read_odometer (itself):
"" "This method prints a specific statement that shows the mileage of the car." ""
print ("This Motorbike has run" + str (self.odometer_reading) + "miles.")
my_bike = Motorcycle ('BMW', 'B7', 2012)
print (my_bike.get_descriptive_name ())
my_bike.odometer_reading = 25
my_bike.read_odometer ()
============== RESTART: C: \ Users \ saifia computers \ Desktop \ Python.py ==============
Bmw B7 from 2012
This motorcycle has run 25 miles.
```

>>>

I finally added a new line of the code. You can see that. Now we move on to the practical. You can add the mileage and get new results. For example, the engine runs for about 20 miles. You will need to add the extra 20 miles into the code to display the new results.

```
Class Motor ():
"" "This is a simple attempt to make a motorcycle." ""
def _init _ (self, company, model, year):
"" "Initializes a set of attributes to describe a car." ""
self.company = company
self.model = model
self.year = year
self.odometer_reading = 0

def get_descriptive_name (itself):
Return a neatly formatted descriptive name. ""
long_name = str (self.year) + '' + self.company + '' + self.model
return long_name.title ()
def read_odometer (itself):
"" "This method prints a specific statement that shows the mileage of the car." ""
print ("This Motorbike has run" + str (self.odometer_reading) + "miles.")
my_bike = Motorcycle ('BMW', 'B7', 2012)
print (my_bike.get_descriptive_name ())
my_bike.odometer_reading = 25 + 20
my_bike.read_odometer ()
============== RESTART: C: \ Users \ saifia computers \ Desktop \ Python.py ==============
Bmw B7 from 2012
This motorcycle has run 45 miles.
>>>
```

You can see that I added a simple Python edit (+) in the code to add the extra miles. It keeps piling up as you add more miles. You can also add multiplication to the code.

```
Class Motor ():
"" "This is a simple attempt to make a motorcycle." ""
def _init _ (self, company, model, year):
"" "Initializes a set of attributes to describe a car." ""
self.company = company
self.model = model
self.year = year
self.odometer_reading = 0

def get_descriptive_name (itself):
Return a neatly formatted descriptive name. ""
long_name = str (self.year) + " + self.company + " + self.model
return long_name.title ()
def read_odometer (itself):
"" "This method prints a specific statement that shows the mileage of the car." ""
print ("This Motorbike has run" + str (self.odometer_reading) + "miles.")
my_bike = Motorcycle ('BMW', 'B7', 2012)
print (my_bike.get_descriptive_name ())
my_bike.odometer_reading = (25 + 20) * 2
my_bike.read_odometer ()
============== RESTART: C: \ Users \ saifia computers \ Desktop \ Python.py ==============
Bmw B7 from 2012
This motorcycle has run 90 miles.
>>>
```

We can add more engines to this class to make it a bit more complicated. I'll add more instances in class to see how it works.

```
Class Motor ():
```

```python
"" "This is a simple attempt to make a motorcycle." ""
def __init__ (self, company, model, year):
"" "Initializes a set of attributes to describe a car." ""
self.company = company
self.model = model
self.year = year
self.odometer_reading = 0
def get_descriptive_name (itself):
Return a neatly formatted descriptive name. ""
long_name = str (self.year) + '' + self.company + '' + self.model
return long_name.title ()
def read_odometer (itself):
"" "This method prints a specific statement that shows the
mileage of the car." ""
print ("This Motorbike has run" + str (self.odometer_reading) +
"miles.")
my_bike = Motorcycle ('BMW', 'B7', 2012)
print (my_bike.get_descriptive_name ())
my_bike.odometer_reading = 100
my_bike.read_odometer ()
my_bike1 = Motorcycle ('Harley Davidson', 'H4', 2020)
print (my_bike1.get_descriptive_name ())
my_bike1.odometer_reading = 500
my_bike1.read_odometer ()
my_bike2 = Engine ('Suzuki', 'S7', 2011)
print (my_fiets2.get_descriptive_name ())
my_bike2.odometer_reading = 1000
my_bike2.read_odometer ()
my_bike3 = Motor ('Triumph', 'T5', 2004)
print (my_bike3.get_descriptive_name ())
my_bike3.odometer_reading = 1500
my_bike3.read_odometer ()
```

```
============== RESTART: C: \ Users \ saifia computers \
Desktop \ Python.py ==============
Bmw B7 from 2012
This motorcycle has run 100 miles.
Harley Davidson H4 from 2020
This motorcycle has run 500 miles.
Suzuki S7 from 2011
This motorcycle has run 1000 miles.
2004 Triumph T5
This motorcycle has run 1500 miles.
>>>
```

This way, you can keep adding different types of bikes along with their mileage. You can add the same type of bikes in the class by assigning them the index number.

If you own a motorcycle showroom or want to open one, you can change the code to make it impossible for employees to reverse the odometer value. As a showroom owner, you need to show your customer the exact product you have. You can put a stop on the mileage after you calculate it. It can go up, but cannot be reversed. This can discourage any attempt by your staff to mislead the customer into making extra money.

```
Class Motor ():
"" "This is a simple attempt to make a motorcycle." ""
def __init __ (self, company, model, year):
"" "Initializes a set of attributes to describe a car." ""
self.company = company
self.model = model
self.year = year
self.odometer_reading = 0

def get_descriptive_name (itself):
Return a neatly formatted descriptive name. ""
long_name = str (self.year) + '' + self.company + '' + self.model
```

```python
        return long_name.title ()
    def read_odometer (itself):
        "" "This method prints a specific statement that shows the
mileage of the car." ""
        print ("This Motorbike has run" + str (self.odometer_reading) +
"miles.")
    def update_odometer (itself, totalMileage):
        "" "this will set the reading to the value you give it and will be
rejected if someone tries to reverse the odometer reading." ""
        if totalMileage> = self.odometer_reading:
            self.odometer_reading = totalMileage
        different:
            print ("Do not try to turn the odometer back. Back off.")

my_bike = Motorcycle ('BMW', 'B7', 2012)
print (my_bike.get_descriptive_name ())
my_bike.odometer_reading = 100
my_bike.read_odometer ()
my_bike.update_odometer (90)
my_bike.read_odometer ()
my_bike1 = Motorcycle ('Harley Davidson', 'H4', 2020)
print (my_bike1.get_descriptive_name ())
my_bike1.odometer_reading = 500
my_bike1.read_odometer ()
my_bike1.update_odometer (600)
my_bike1.read_odometer ()
my_bike2 = Engine ('Suzuki', 'S7', 2011)
print (my_fiets2.get_descriptive_name ())
my_bike2.odometer_reading = 1000
my_bike2.read_odometer ()
my_bike2.update_odometer (999)
my_bike2.read_odometer ()
my_bike3 = Motor ('Triumph', 'T5', 2004)
```

```
print (my_bike3.get_descriptive_name ())
my_bike3.odometer_reading = 1500
my_bike3.read_odometer ()
my_bike3.update_odometer (1400)
my_bike3.read_odometer ()
============== RESTART: C: \ Users \ saifia computers \ Desktop \ Python.py ==============
Bmw B7 from 2012
This motorcycle has run 100 miles.
Do not try to turn the odometer back. Piss off.
This motorcycle has run 100 miles.
Harley Davidson H4 from 2020
This motorcycle has run 500 miles.
This motorcycle has run 600 miles.
Suzuki S7 from 2011
This motorcycle has run 1000 miles.
Do not try to turn the odometer back. Piss off.
This motorcycle has run 1000 miles.
2004 Triumph T5
This motorcycle has run 1500 miles.
Do not try to turn the odometer back. Piss off.
This motorcycle has run 1500 miles.
>>>
```

I have added the update function in the code. Now, the amount you set for each bike can in no way be reversed. It keeps displaying the message no matter how many times your employees try to roll it back.

Increase an attribute

There will come a time when you may need to increase the value of an attribute to some degree. You may also feel the need to set an entirely new value. Supposing you buy a new engine and you want to calculate the mileage you run before registering it, you can do this by adding a simple method to the code.

```
Class Motor ():
"" "This is a simple attempt to make a motorcycle." ""
def _init _ (self, company, model, year):
"" "Initializes a set of attributes to describe a car." ""
self.company = company
self.model = model
self.year = year
self.odometer_reading = 0


def get_descriptive_name (itself):
Return a neatly formatted descriptive name. ""
long_name = str (self.year) + '' + self.company + '' + self.model
return long_name.title ()
def read_odometer (itself):
"" "This method prints a specific statement that shows the
mileage of the car." ""
print ("This Motorbike has run" + str (self.odometer_reading) +
"miles.")
def update_odometer (itself, totalMileage):
"" "this will set the reading to the value you give it and will be
rejected if someone tries to reverse the odometer reading." ""
if totalMileage> = self.odometer_reading:
self.odometer_reading = totalMileage
different:
print ("Do not try to turn the odometer back. Back off.")
def increment_odometer (itself, miles):
```

You can add the specified amount to the existing value. ""
self.odometer_reading + = miles


```
my_bike = Motorcycle ('BMW', 'B7', 2012)
print (my_bike.get_descriptive_name ())
my_bike.update_odometer (90)
my_bike.read_odometer ()
my_bike.increment_odometer (200)
my_bike.read_odometer ()
my_bike1 = Motorcycle ('Harley Davidson', 'H4', 2020)
print (my_bike1.get_descriptive_name ())
my_bike1.update_odometer (600)
my_bike1.read_odometer ()
my_bike.increment_odometer (100)
my_bike.read_odometer ()
my_bike2 = Engine ('Suzuki', 'S7', 2011)
print (my_fiets2.get_descriptive_name ())
my_bike2.update_odometer (999)
my_bike2.read_odometer ()
my_bike.increment_odometer (200)
my_bike.read_odometer ()
my_bike3 = Motor ('Triumph', 'T5', 2004)
print (my_bike3.get_descriptive_name ())
my_bike3.update_odometer (1400)
my_bike3.read_odometer ()
my_bike.increment_odometer (1000)
my_bike.read_odometer ()
============== RESTART: C: \ Users \ saifia computers \
Desktop \ Python.py ==============
Bmw B7 from 2012
This motorcycle has run 90 miles.
This motorcycle has run 290 miles.
Harley Davidson H4 from 2020
```

This motorcycle has run 600 miles.
This motorcycle has run 390 miles.
Suzuki S7 from 2011
This motorcycle has run 999 miles.
This motorcycle has run 590 miles.
2004 Triumph T5
This motorcycle has run 1400 miles.
This motorcycle has run 1590 miles.
>>>

The increment_odometer method takes the number of miles as input and adds it to the self.odometer_reading. The program performed well on the first engine and increased the mileage. It took the reading of the first car and increased the rest of the cars that caused aberration in the mileage on the odometer. It is best to use a single motor to fill it in with values.

The Child Class

We can add an electric bike to the parent Motorbike class. The children's class for the electric bicycle needs attributes of the parent class. This will be a new model, but will inherit the values from the parent class with the title Motorbike.

Class Motor ():
"" "This is a simple attempt to make a motorcycle." ""
def __init __ (self, company, model, year):
"" "Initializes a set of attributes to describe a car." ""
self.company = company
self.model = model
self.year = year
self.odometer_reading = 0

def get_descriptive_name (itself):
Return a neatly formatted descriptive name. ""
long_name = str (self.year) + '' + self.company + '' + self.model
return long_name.title ()

```python
def read_odometer (itself):
"" "This method prints a specific statement that shows the
mileage of the car." ""
print ("This Motorbike has run" + str (self.odometer_reading) +
"miles.")
def update_odometer (itself, totalMileage):
"" "this will set the reading to the value you give it and will be
rejected if someone tries to reverse the odometer reading." ""
if totalMileage> = self.odometer_reading:
self.odometer_reading = totalMileage
different:
print ("Do not try to turn the odometer back. Back off.")
def increment_odometer (itself, miles):
You can add the specified amount to the existing value. ""
self.odometer_reading + = miles
Class ElectricMotorbike (Motorbike):
"" "This represents all aspects of the parent class." ""
def _init _ (self, company, model, year):
Starts the attributes of the parent class. ""
super () ._ init _ (company, model, year)


my_bike = Motorcycle ('BMW', 'B7', 2012)
print (my_bike.get_descriptive_name ())
my_bike.update_odometer (90)
my_bike.read_odometer ()
my_bike.increment_odometer (200)
my_bike.read_odometer ()
my_bike1 = Motorcycle ('Harley Davidson', 'H4', 2020)
print (my_bike1.get_descriptive_name ())
my_bike1.update_odometer (600)
my_bike1.read_odometer ()
my_bike.increment_odometer (100)
my_bike.read_odometer ()
```

```
my_bike2 = Engine ('Suzuki', 'S7', 2011)
print (my_fiets2.get_descriptive_name ())
my_bike2.update_odometer (999)
my_bike2.read_odometer ()
my_bike.increment_odometer (200)
my_bike.read_odometer ()
my_bike3 = Motor ('Triumph', 'T5', 2004)
print (my_bike3.get_descriptive_name ())
my_bike3.update_odometer (1400)
my_bike3.read_odometer ()
my_bike.increment_odometer (1000)
my_bike.read_odometer ()
my_yamaha = ElectricMotorbike ('Yamaha', 'x model', 2019)
print (my_yamaha.get_descriptive_name ())
============== RESTART: C: \ Users \ saifia computers \
Desktop \ Python.py =============
Bmw B7 from 2012
This motorcycle has run 90 miles.
This motorcycle has run 290 miles.
Harley Davidson H4 from 2020
This motorcycle has run 600 miles.
This motorcycle has run 390 miles.
Suzuki S7 from 2011
This motorcycle has run 999 miles.
This motorcycle has run 590 miles.
2004 Triumph T5
This motorcycle has run 1400 miles.
This motorcycle has run 1590 miles.
2019 Yamaha X model
>>>
```

We start at the tail of the big league. In order to inherit the attributes of the parent class, the child class must be written within the parent class. You must enclose the parent class name in parentheses. The __init__ () method gets the information needed to create the auto instance. Next comes the super () function, a special function that helps Python in the association between the child and its parent. Super refers to the parent class according to the Python tradition, while the child class is named as a subclass.

In the following example, I transfer the attributes from the parent class to the child class. I will also add an engine in the children's class. See how easily and smoothly the child class incorporates the features of the parent class.

```python
Class Motor ():
"" "This is a simple attempt to make a motorcycle." ""
def __init__ (self, company, model, year):
"" "Initializes a set of attributes to describe a car." ""
self.company = company
self.model = model
self.year = year
self.odometer_reading = 0

def get_descriptive_name (itself):
Return a neatly formatted descriptive name. ""
long_name = str (self.year) + " + self.company + " + self.model
return long_name.title ()
def read_odometer (itself):
"" "This method prints a specific statement that shows the mileage of the car." ""
print ("This Motorbike has run" + str (self.odometer_reading) + "miles.")
def update_odometer (itself, totalMileage):
```

```python
"" "this will set the reading to the value you give it and will be
rejected if someone tries to reverse the odometer reading." ""
if totalMileage> = self.odometer_reading:
self.odometer_reading = totalMileage
different:
print ("Do not try to turn the odometer back. Back off.")
def increment_odometer (itself, miles):
You can add the specified amount to the existing value. ""
self.odometer_reading + = miles
Class ElectricMotorbike (Motorbike):
"" "This represents all aspects of the parent class." ""
def _init _ (self, company, model, year):
Starts the attributes of the parent class. ""
super () ._ init _ (company, model, year)


my_bike = Motorcycle ('BMW', 'B7', 2012)
print (my_bike.get_descriptive_name ())
my_bike.update_odometer (90)
my_bike.read_odometer ()
my_bike.increment_odometer (200)
my_bike.read_odometer ()
my_yamaha = ElectricMotorbike ('Yamaha', 'x model', 2019)
print (my_yamaha.get_descriptive_name ())
my_yamaha.update_odometer (90)
my_yamaha.read_odometer ()
my_yamaha.increment_odometer (300)
my_yamaha.read_odometer ()
my_yamaha1 = ElectricMotorbike ('Yamaha', 'z model', 2009)
print (my_yamaha.get_descriptive_name ())
my_yamaha1.update_odometer (100)
my_yamaha1.read_odometer ()
my_yamaha1.increment_odometer (100)
my_yamaha1.read_odometer ()
```

```
============== RESTART: C: \ Users \ saifia computers \
Desktop \ Python.py ==============
Bmw B7 from 2012
This motorcycle has run 90 miles.
This motorcycle has run 290 miles.
2019 Yamaha X model
This motorcycle has run 90 miles.
This motorcycle has run 390 miles.
2019 Yamaha X model
This motorcycle has run 100 miles.
This motorcycle has run 200 miles.
>>>
```

Map individual attributes to the child class

You saw how I added attributes to the parent class, and then transferred them to the child class. Now it is time to see how you can add separate attributes to the child class. A special feature of the parent class is that the characteristics of the child class are not transferred to the parent class. Let's see how it works.

I will keep one instance of the parent class and add two instances to the child's class. The child class has separate attributes that are not transferred to the parent class, while the characteristics of the parent class are inherited.

```python
Class Motor ():
"" "This is a simple attempt to make a motorcycle." ""
def __init__ (self, company, model, year):
"" "Initializes a set of attributes to describe a car." ""
self.company = company
self.model = model
self.year = year
self.odometer_reading = 0
```

```python
def get_descriptive_name (itself):
Return a neatly formatted descriptive name. ""
long_name = str (self.year) + '' + self.company + '' + self.model
return long_name.title ()
def read_odometer (itself):
"" "This method prints a specific statement that shows the
mileage of the car." ""
print ("This Motorbike has run" + str (self.odometer_reading) +
"miles.")
def update_odometer (itself, totalMileage):
"" "this will set the reading to the value you give it and will be
rejected if someone tries to reverse the odometer reading." ""
if totalMileage> = self.odometer_reading:
self.odometer_reading = totalMileage
different:
print ("Do not try to turn the odometer back. Back off.")
def increment_odometer (itself, miles):
You can add the specified amount to the existing value. ""
self.odometer_reading + = miles
Class ElectricMotorbike (Motorbike):
"" "This represents all aspects of the parent class." ""
def __init __ (self, company, model, year):
Starts the attributes of the parent class. ""
super () ._ init __ (company, model, year)
self.color_type = 'red hot'
def description_color (itself):
print ("This engine is from" + str (self.color_type) + "color.")

my_bike = Motorcycle ('BMW', 'B7', 2012)
print (my_bike.get_descriptive_name ())
my_bike.update_odometer (90)
my_bike.read_odometer ()
```

```python
my_bike.increment_odometer (200)
my_bike.read_odometer ()
my_yamaha = ElectricMotorbike ('Yamaha', 'x model', 2019)
print (my_yamaha.get_descriptive_name ())
my_yamaha.describe_color ()
my_yamaha.update_odometer (90)
my_yamaha.read_odometer ()
my_yamaha.increment_odometer (300)
my_yamaha.read_odometer ()
my_yamaha1 = ElectricMotorbike ('Yamaha', 'z model', 2009)
print (my_yamaha.get_descriptive_name ())
my_yamaha.describe_color ()
my_yamaha1.update_odometer (100)
my_yamaha1.read_odometer ()
my_yamaha1.increment_odometer (100)
my_yamaha1.read_odometer ()
============== RESTART: C: \ Users \ saifia computers \
Desktop \ Python.py =============
Bmw B7 from 2012
This motorcycle has run 90 miles.
This motorcycle has run 290 miles.
2019 Yamaha X model
This engine has a red hot color.
This motorcycle has run 90 miles.
This motorcycle has run 390 miles.
2019 Yamaha X model
This engine has a red hot color.
This motorcycle has run 100 miles.
This motorcycle has run 200 miles.
>>>
```

You can see I added a new attribute called self.color_type to the underlying class. This is just an example; therefore it is limited in size. You can add as many attributes to the child class as you need.

Ignore it

You can see that the child class has all the attributes of the parent class by default. What if this is something bad for you? What if you don't need it? What if you need to omit the descriptive name from the kids' class because you don't want to show it to your customer visiting your online store? There is a method to override each attribute of the parent class. You have to add another line of code to the classes.

Class Motor ():
"" "This is a simple attempt to make a motorcycle." ""
def _init _ (self, company, model, year):
"" "Initializes a set of attributes to describe a car." ""
self.company = company
self.model = model
self.year = year
self.odometer_reading = 0

def get_descriptive_name (itself):
Return a neatly formatted descriptive name. ""
long_name = str (self.year) + '' + self.company + '' + self.model
return long_name.title ()
def read_odometer (itself):
"" "This method prints a specific statement that shows the mileage of the car." ""
print ("This Motorbike has run" + str (self.odometer_reading) + "miles.")
def update_odometer (itself, totalMileage):
"" "this will set the reading to the value you give it and will be rejected if someone tries to reverse the odometer reading." ""

```python
if totalMileage> = self.odometer_reading:
self.odometer_reading = totalMileage
different:
print ("Do not try to turn the odometer back. Back off.")
def increment_odometer (itself, miles):
You can add the specified amount to the existing value. ""
self.odometer_reading + = miles
Class ElectricMotorbike (Motorbike):
"" "This represents all aspects of the parent class." ""
def _init _ (self, company, model, year):
Starts the attributes of the parent class. ""
super () ._ init _ (company, model, year)
self.color_type = 'red hot'
def description_color (itself):
print ("This engine is from" + str (self.color_type) + "color.")
def get_descriptive_name (itself):
print ("This is not required for electric cars.")


my_bike = Motorcycle ('BMW', 'B7', 2012)
print (my_bike.get_descriptive_name ())
my_bike.update_odometer (90)
my_bike.read_odometer ()
my_bike.increment_odometer (200)
my_bike.read_odometer ()
my_yamaha = ElectricMotorbike ('Yamaha', 'x model', 2019)
print (my_yamaha.get_descriptive_name ())
my_yamaha.describe_color ()
my_yamaha.update_odometer (90)
my_yamaha.read_odometer ()
my_yamaha.increment_odometer (300)
my_yamaha.read_odometer ()
my_yamaha1 = ElectricMotorbike ('Yamaha', 'z model', 2009)
print (my_yamaha.get_descriptive_name ())
```

my_yamaha.describe_color ()
my_yamaha1.update_odometer (100)
my_yamaha1.read_odometer ()
my_yamaha1.increment_odometer (100)
my_yamaha1.read_odometer ()
============== RESTART: C: \ Users \ saifia computers \
Desktop \ Python.py ==============
Bmw B7 from 2012
This motorcycle has run 90 miles.
This motorcycle has run 290 miles.
This is not required for electric cars.
No
This engine has a red hot color.
This motorcycle has run 90 miles.
This motorcycle has run 390 miles.
This is not required for electric cars.
No
This engine has a red hot color.
This motorcycle has run 100 miles.
This motorcycle has run 200 miles.
>>>
In the following code snippet, I will remove all the attributes
from the parent class and you can only see the results of the
attributes specific to the child class.
Class Motor ():
"" "This is a simple attempt to make a motorcycle." ""
def _init _ (self, company, model, year):
"" "Initializes a set of attributes to describe a car." ""
self.company = company
self.model = model
self.year = year
self.odometer_reading = 0

```python
def get_descriptive_name (itself):
Return a neatly formatted descriptive name. ""
long_name = str (self.year) + " + self.company + " + self.model
return long_name.title ()
def read_odometer (itself):
"" "This method prints a specific statement that shows the
mileage of the car." ""
print ("This Motorbike has run" + str (self.odometer_reading) +
"miles.")
def update_odometer (itself, totalMileage):
"" "this will set the reading to the value you give it and will be
rejected if someone tries to reverse the odometer reading." ""
if totalMileage> = self.odometer_reading:
self.odometer_reading = totalMileage
different:
print ("Do not try to turn the odometer back. Back off.")
def increment_odometer (itself, miles):
You can add the specified amount to the existing value. ""
self.odometer_reading + = miles
Class ElectricMotorbike (Motorbike):
"" "This represents all aspects of the parent class." ""
def _init _ (self, company, model, year):
Starts the attributes of the parent class. ""
super () ._ init _ (company, model, year)
self.color_type = 'red hot'
def description_color (itself):
print ("This engine is from" + str (self.color_type) + "color.")
def get_descriptive_name (itself):
print ("This is not required for electric cars.")
def read_odometer (itself):
print ("This is not required for electric cars.")
def update_odometer (itself, totalMileage):
print ("This is not required for electric cars.")
```

```python
def increment_odometer (itself, miles):
print ("This is not required for electric cars.")
my_yamaha = ElectricMotorbike ('Yamaha', 'x model', 2019)
print (my_yamaha.get_descriptive_name ())
my_yamaha.describe_color ()
my_yamaha.update_odometer (90)
my_yamaha.read_odometer ()
my_yamaha.increment_odometer (300)
my_yamaha.read_odometer ()
my_yamaha1 = ElectricMotorbike ('Yamaha', 'z model', 2009)
print (my_yamaha.get_descriptive_name ())
my_yamaha.describe_color ()
my_yamaha1.update_odometer (100)
my_yamaha1.read_odometer ()
my_yamaha1.increment_odometer (100)
my_yamaha1.read_odometer ()
============== RESTART: C: \ Users \ saifia computers \
Desktop \ Python.py =============
This is not required for electric cars.
No
This engine has a red hot color.
This is not required for electric cars.
This is not required for electric cars.
This is not required for electric cars.
This is not required for electric cars.
This is not required for electric cars.
No
This engine has a red hot color.
This is not required for electric cars.
This is not required for electric cars.
This is not required for electric cars.
This is not required for electric cars.
>>>
```

If you are about to build a complex project that requires you to enter a lot of details about an electric motor, you can proceed to create a separate class for each detail. All additional classes can be modified in the code as child classes that would support the parent class. In the previous example, I added the color of the engine in the existing kids class. In the following example I am going to create a new kids class for the color of the electric motor.

```
Class Motor ():
"" "This is a simple attempt to make a motorcycle." ""
def _init _ (self, company, model, year):
"" "Initializes a set of attributes to describe a car." ""
self.company = company
self.model = model
self.year = year
self.odometer_reading = 0


def get_descriptive_name (itself):
Return a neatly formatted descriptive name. ""
long_name = str (self.year) + '' + self.company + '' + self.model
return long_name.title ()
def read_odometer (itself):
"" "This method prints a specific statement that shows the mileage of the car." ""
print ("This Motorbike has run" + str (self.odometer_reading) + "miles.")
def update_odometer (itself, totalMileage):
"" "this will set the reading to the value you give it and will be rejected if someone tries to reverse the odometer reading." ""
if totalMileage> = self.odometer_reading:
self.odometer_reading = totalMileage
different:
print ("Do not try to turn the odometer back. Back off.")
```

def increment_odometer (itself, miles):
You can add the specified amount to the existing value. ""
self.odometer_reading + = miles
Class Color ():
def _init _ (self, color_type = 'red hot'):
self.color_type = color type
def description_color (itself):
print ("This engine is from" + str (self.color_type) + "color.")

Class ElectricMotorbike (Motorbike):
"" "This represents all aspects of the parent class." ""
def _init _ (self, company, model, year):
Starts the attributes of the parent class. ""
super () ._ init _ (company, model, year)
self.color = Color ()
my_yamaha = ElectricMotorbike ('Yamaha', 'x model', 2019)
print (my_yamaha.get_descriptive_name ())
my_yamaha.color.describe_color ()
my_yamaha.update_odometer (90)
my_yamaha.read_odometer ()
my_yamaha.increment_odometer (300)
my_yamaha.read_odometer ()
my_yamaha1 = ElectricMotorbike ('Yamaha', 'z model', 2009)
print (my_yamaha.get_descriptive_name ())
my_yamaha.color.describe_color ()
my_yamaha1.update_odometer (100)
my_yamaha1.read_odometer ()
my_yamaha1.increment_odometer (100)
my_yamaha1.read_odometer ()
============== RESTART: C: \ Users \ saifia computers \
Desktop \ Python.py =============
2019 Yamaha X model
This engine has a red hot color.

This motorcycle has run 90 miles.
This motorcycle has run 390 miles.
2019 Yamaha X model
This engine has a red hot color.
This motorcycle has run 100 miles.
This motorcycle has run 200 miles.
>>>

How to import a class?

I'm going to create a module that would contain the Motorbike class. Make sure the filename is unique for the parent and child class. You can store the motor class in a module that you can name as motorbike.py. The following code must be placed in a separate file.

```python
Class Motor ():
"" "This is a simple attempt to make a motorcycle." ""
def __init __ (self, company, model, year):
"" "Initializes a set of attributes to describe a car." ""
self.company = company
self.model = model
self.year = year
self.odometer_reading = 0

def get_descriptive_name (itself):
Return a neatly formatted descriptive name. ""
long_name = str (self.year) + '' + self.company + '' + self.model
return long_name.title ()
def read_odometer (itself):
"" "This method prints a specific statement that shows the mileage of the car." ""
print ("This Motorbike has run" + str (self.odometer_reading) + "miles.")
def update_odometer (itself, totalMileage):
```

"" "this will set the reading to the value you give it, and it will be rejected if someone tries to reverse the odometer reading." ""

if totalMileage> = self.odometer_reading:

self.odometer_reading = totalMileage

different:

print ("Do not try to turn the odometer back. Back off.")

def increment_odometer (itself, miles):

You can add the specified amount to the existing value. ""

self.odometer_reading + = miles

This is the code to save as motorbike.py in the same location where you need to save the other file. Now we are going to create a second file containing the child class. In the very first line of the code I will import the parent class. It is not necessary to write the complete code in the second file. I will import the module and the child class will use the attributes.

from motor import Motorbike

Class Color ():

def _init _ (self, color_type = 'red hot'):

self.color_type = color type

def description_color (itself):

print ("This engine is from" + str (self.color_type) + "color.")

Class ElectricMotorbike (Motorbike):

"" "This represents all aspects of the parent class." ""

def _init _ (self, company, model, year):

Starts the attributes of the parent class. ""

super () ._ init _ (company, model, year)

self.color = Color ()

my_yamaha = ElectricMotorbike ('Yamaha', 'x model', 2019)

print (my_yamaha.get_descriptive_name ())

my_yamaha.color.describe_color ()

my_yamaha.update_odometer (90)

my_yamaha.read_odometer ()

```
my_yamaha.increment_odometer (300)
my_yamaha.read_odometer ()
my_yamaha1 = ElectricMotorbike ('Yamaha', 'z model', 2009)
print (my_yamaha.get_descriptive_name ())
my_yamaha.color.describe_color ()
my_yamaha1.update_odometer (100)
my_yamaha1.read_odometer ()
my_yamaha1.increment_odometer (100)
my_yamaha1.read_odometer ()
============== RESTART: C: \ Users \ saifia computers \
Desktop \ Python.py ==============
2019 Yamaha X model
This engine has a red hot color.
This motorcycle has run 90 miles.
This motorcycle has run 390 miles.
2019 Yamaha X model
This engine has a red hot color.
This motorcycle has run 100 miles.
This motorcycle has run 200 miles.
>>>
```

In the above module, I saved a single class in the file. You can save multiple classes in one file and then import them separately. Let's see how to do that. The file named engine contains the following classes:

```
Class Motor ():
"" "This is a simple attempt to make a motorcycle." ""
def _init _ (self, company, model, year):
"" "Initializes a set of attributes to describe a car." ""
self.company = company
self.model = model
self.year = year
self.odometer_reading = 0
```

def get_descriptive_name (itself):
Return a neatly formatted descriptive name. ""
long_name = str (self.year) + " + self.company + " + self.model
return long_name.title ()
def read_odometer (itself):
"" "This method prints a specific statement that shows the
mileage of the car." ""
print ("This Motorbike has run" + str (self.odometer_reading) +
"miles.")
def update_odometer (itself, totalMileage):
"" "this will set the reading to the value you give it and will be
rejected if someone tries to reverse the odometer reading." ""
if totalMileage> = self.odometer_reading:
self.odometer_reading = totalMileage
different:
print ("Do not try to turn the odometer back. Back off.")
def increment_odometer (itself, miles):
You can add the specified amount to the existing value. ""
self.odometer_reading + = miles
Class Color ():
def _init _ (self, color_type = 'red hot'):
self.color_type = color type
def description_color (itself):
print ("This engine is from" + str (self.color_type) + "color.")

Class ElectricMotorbike (Motorbike):
"" "This represents all aspects of the parent class." ""
def _init _ (self, company, model, year):
Starts the attributes of the parent class. ""
super () ._ init _ (company, model, year)
self.color = Color ()
In the following code examples, I will import all three classes
separately to see how they affect the program.

```python
from motor import Motorbike
my_bike = Motorcycle ('BMW', 'B7', 2012)
print (my_bike.get_descriptive_name ())
my_bike.update_odometer (90)
my_bike.read_odometer ()
my_bike.increment_odometer (200)
my_bike.read_odometer ()
my_bike1 = Motorcycle ('Harley Davidson', 'H4', 2020)
print (my_bike1.get_descriptive_name ())
my_bike1.update_odometer (600)
my_bike1.read_odometer ()
my_bike.increment_odometer (100)
my_bike.read_odometer ()
my_yamaha = ElectricMotorbike ('Yamaha', 'x model', 2019)
print (my_yamaha.get_descriptive_name ())
my_yamaha.color.describe_color ()
my_yamaha.update_odometer (90)
my_yamaha.read_odometer ()
my_yamaha.increment_odometer (300)
my_yamaha.read_odometer ()
my_yamaha1 = ElectricMotorbike ('Yamaha', 'z model', 2009)
print (my_yamaha.get_descriptive_name ())
my_yamaha.color.describe_color ()
my_yamaha1.update_odometer (100)
my_yamaha1.read_odometer ()
my_yamaha1.increment_odometer (100)
my_yamaha1.read_odometer ()
============== RESTART: C: \ Users \ saifia computers \
Desktop \ Python.py =============
Bmw B7 from 2012
This motorcycle has run 90 miles.
This motorcycle has run 290 miles.
Harley Davidson H4 from 2020
```

This motorcycle has run 600 miles.
This motorcycle has run 390 miles.
Retrace (most recent call last)
File "C: \ Users \ saifia computers \ Desktop \ Python.py", line 22, in <module>
my_yamaha = ElectricMotorbike ('Yamaha', 'x model', 2019)
NameError: name 'ElectricMotorbike' is not defined
>>>
You can see that the program ran well with regard to the attributes of the parent class. When it came to the child class, it resulted in an error. In the following code example, I import the second class.

```
from motor import ElectricMotorbike
my_yamaha = ElectricMotorbike ('Yamaha', 'x model', 2019)
print (my_yamaha.get_descriptive_name ())
my_yamaha.color.describe_color ()
my_yamaha.update_odometer (90)
my_yamaha.read_odometer ()
my_yamaha.increment_odometer (300)
my_yamaha.read_odometer ()
my_yamaha1 = ElectricMotorbike ('Yamaha', 'z model', 2009)
print (my_yamaha.get_descriptive_name ())
my_yamaha.color.describe_color ()
my_yamaha1.update_odometer (100)
my_yamaha1.read_odometer ()
my_yamaha1.increment_odometer (100)
my_yamaha1.read_odometer ()
============== RESTART: C: \ Users \ saifia computers \ Desktop \ Python.py ==============
2019 Yamaha X model
This engine has a red hot color.
This motorcycle has run 90 miles.
This motorcycle has run 390 miles.
```

2019 Yamaha X model
This engine has a red hot color.
This motorcycle has run 100 miles.
This motorcycle has run 200 miles.
>>>
Now the third class comes out of the module.
from motor import Color
my_yamaha = ElectricMotorbike ('Yamaha', 'x model', 2019)
print (my_yamaha.get_descriptive_name ())
my_yamaha.color.describe_color ()
my_yamaha.update_odometer (90)
my_yamaha.read_odometer ()
my_yamaha.increment_odometer (300)
my_yamaha.read_odometer ()
my_yamaha1 = ElectricMotorbike ('Yamaha', 'z model', 2009)
print (my_yamaha.get_descriptive_name ())
my_yamaha.color.describe_color ()
my_yamaha1.update_odometer (100)
my_yamaha1.read_odometer ()
my_yamaha1.increment_odometer (100)
my_yamaha1.read_odometer ()
============== RESTART: C: \ Users \ saifia computers \
Desktop \ Python.py =============
Retrace (most recent call last)
File "C: \ Users \ saifia computers \ Desktop \ Python.py", line 3,
in <module>
my_yamaha = ElectricMotorbike ('Yamaha', 'x model', 2019)
NameError: name 'ElectricMotorbike' is not defined
>>>
This returned an error because the color does not match the attributes. We also need to import the ElecricMotorbike class for the program to run smoothly. Yes, we can import two classes at the same time.

```
from motor import ElectricMotorbike
from motor import Color
my_yamaha = ElectricMotorbike ('Yamaha', 'x model', 2019)
print (my_yamaha.get_descriptive_name ())
my_yamaha.color.describe_color ()
my_yamaha.update_odometer (90)
my_yamaha.read_odometer ()
my_yamaha.increment_odometer (300)
my_yamaha.read_odometer ()
my_yamaha1 = ElectricMotorbike ('Yamaha', 'z model', 2009)
print (my_yamaha.get_descriptive_name ())
my_yamaha.color.describe_color ()
my_yamaha1.update_odometer (100)
my_yamaha1.read_odometer ()
my_yamaha1.increment_odometer (100)
my_yamaha1.read_odometer ()
============== RESTART: C: \ Users \ saifia computers \
Desktop \ Python.py =============
2019 Yamaha X model
This engine has a red hot color.
This motorcycle has run 90 miles.
This motorcycle has run 390 miles.
2019 Yamaha X model
This engine has a red hot color.
This motorcycle has run 100 miles.
This motorcycle has run 200 miles.
>>>
```

Now the code runs smoothly. In the following example, I import
the entire module, which means I import all three classes at
once.

```
from motor import Motorbike
from motor import ElectricMotorbike
from motor import Color
```

```
my_bike = Motorcycle ('BMW', 'B7', 2012)
print (my_bike.get_descriptive_name ())
my_bike.update_odometer (90)
my_bike.read_odometer ()
my_bike.increment_odometer (200)
my_bike.read_odometer ()
my_bike1 = Motorcycle ('Harley Davidson', 'H4', 2020)
print (my_bike1.get_descriptive_name ())
my_bike1.update_odometer (600)
my_bike1.read_odometer ()
my_bike.increment_odometer (100)
my_bike.read_odometer ()
my_yamaha = ElectricMotorbike ('Yamaha', 'x model', 2019)
print (my_yamaha.get_descriptive_name ())
my_yamaha.color.describe_color ()
my_yamaha.update_odometer (90)
my_yamaha.read_odometer ()
my_yamaha.increment_odometer (300)
my_yamaha.read_odometer ()
my_yamaha1 = ElectricMotorbike ('Yamaha', 'z model', 2009)
print (my_yamaha.get_descriptive_name ())
my_yamaha.color.describe_color ()
my_yamaha1.update_odometer (100)
my_yamaha1.read_odometer ()
my_yamaha1.increment_odometer (100)
my_yamaha1.read_odometer ()
============== RESTART: C: \ Users \ saifia computers \
Desktop \ Python.py =============
Bmw B7 from 2012
This motorcycle has run 90 miles.
This motorcycle has run 290 miles.
Harley Davidson H4 from 2020
This motorcycle has run 600 miles.
```

This motorcycle has run 390 miles.
2019 Yamaha X model
This engine has a red hot color.
This motorcycle has run 90 miles.
This motorcycle has run 390 miles.
2019 Yamaha X model
This engine has a red hot color.
This motorcycle has run 100 miles.
This motorcycle has run 200 miles.
>>>

A very easy way to import all classes from the module is to add an * in the code, just like the following:

```
from motor import *
my_bike = Motorcycle ('BMW', 'B7', 2012)
print (my_bike.get_descriptive_name ())
my_bike.update_odometer (90)
my_bike.read_odometer ()
my_bike.increment_odometer (200)
my_bike.read_odometer ()
my_bike1 = Motorcycle ('Harley Davidson', 'H4', 2020)
print (my_bike1.get_descriptive_name ())
my_bike1.update_odometer (600)
my_bike1.read_odometer ()
my_bike.increment_odometer (100)
my_bike.read_odometer ()
my_yamaha = ElectricMotorbike ('Yamaha', 'x model', 2019)
print (my_yamaha.get_descriptive_name ())
my_yamaha.color.describe_color ()
my_yamaha.update_odometer (90)
my_yamaha.read_odometer ()
my_yamaha.increment_odometer (300)
my_yamaha.read_odometer ()
my_yamaha1 = ElectricMotorbike ('Yamaha', 'z model', 2009)
```

```python
print (my_yamaha.get_descriptive_name ())
my_yamaha.color.describe_color ()
my_yamaha1.update_odometer (100)
my_yamaha1.read_odometer ()
my_yamaha1.increment_odometer (100)
my_yamaha1.read_odometer ()
```

Chapter 7 : Python programs

The first program I'm going to make is a guess with the numbers game. I will import Python's built-in library which is called random. I will give the program a range of 0-50 numbers. The user enters the number of his choice and Python returns the message if a number is higher or lower than the actual number he guessed. When the user enters the correct number, he or she will receive a message of congratulations. The following is the source code for this interesting game.

Guess the number

import randomly

number = random. range (0.50)

recommend Check = "you're wrong."

print ("Dear player, you are welcome at Number Guess")

while guessCheck == "you're wrong":

response = int (input ("You must enter a number between 0 and 50:"))

to attempt:

val = int (response)

except ValueError:

print ("This is an invalid integer. Please try again")

continue

val = int (response)

if val <number:

print ("The number you entered is less than the actual number. Please try again.")

elif val> number:

print ("The number you entered is higher than the actual number. Please try again.")

different:

```
print ("Hurray! You gave the correct answer.")
recommendCheck = "correct"
print ("Thank you, player, for playing this interesting game. See
you soon")
```

============== RESTART: C: \ Users \ saifia computers \ Desktop \ Python.py ==============
Dear player, you are welcome at Number Guess
You must enter a number between 0 and 50: 5
The number you entered is lower than the actual number. You have to try again.
You must enter a number between 0 and 50: 5
The number you entered is lower than the actual number. You have to try again.
You must enter a number between 0 and 50:10
The number you entered is lower than the actual number. You have to try again.
You must enter a number between 0 and 50:15
The number you entered is lower than the actual number. You have to try again.
You must enter a number between 0 and 50:20
The number you entered is lower than the actual number. You have to try again.
You must enter a number between 0 and 50:25
The number you entered is lower than the actual number. You have to try again.
You must enter a number between 0 and 50:30
The number you entered is lower than the actual number. You have to try again.
You must enter a number between 0 and 50:40
The number you entered is higher than the actual number. You have to try again.
You must enter a number between 0 and 50:35
Hoera! You have given the correct answer.

Thanks, player, for playing this interesting game. Bye

```
>>>
```

You can adjust the source code and make it more complex and interesting by increasing the number of digits. You will need to make some changes to the code as under:

```python
import randomly
number = random. range (0,100)
recommend Check = "you're wrong."
print ("Dear player, you are welcome at Number Guess")
while guessCheck == "you're wrong":
response = int (input ("You must enter a number between 0 and 100:"))
to attempt:
val = int (response)
except ValueError:
print ("This is an invalid integer. Please try again")
continue
val = int (response)
if val <number:
print ("The number you entered is less than the actual number. Please try again.")
elif val> number:
print ("The number you entered is higher than the actual number. Please try again.")
different:
print ("Hurray! You gave the correct answer.")
recommendCheck = "correct"
print ("Thank you, player, for playing this interesting game. See you soon")
============== RESTART: C: \ Users \ saifia computers \ Desktop \ Python.py =============
Dear player, you are welcome at Number Guess
You must enter a number between 0 and 100: 10
```

The number you entered is lower than the actual number. You have to try again.
You must enter a number between 0 and 100: 15
The number you entered is lower than the actual number. You have to try again.
You must enter a number between 0 and 100:20
The number you entered is lower than the actual number. You have to try again.
You must enter a number between 0 and 100:20
The number you entered is lower than the actual number. You have to try again.
You must enter a number between 0 and 100:30
The number you entered is lower than the actual number. You have to try again.
You must enter a number between 0 and 100: 35
The number you entered is lower than the actual number. You have to try again.
You must enter a number between 0 and 100:40
The number you entered is lower than the actual number. You have to try again.
You must enter a number between 0 and 100: 50
The number you entered is lower than the actual number. You have to try again.
You must enter a number between 0 and 100: 55
The number you entered is lower than the actual number. You have to try again.
You must enter a number between 0 and 100: 60
The number you entered is lower than the actual number. You have to try again.
You must enter a number between 0 and 100: 65
The number you entered is higher than the actual number. You have to try again.
You must enter a number between 0 and 100: 70

The number you entered is higher than the actual number. You have to try again.
You must enter a number between 0 and 100: 61
Hoera! You have given the correct answer.
Thanks, player, for playing this interesting game. Bye
>>>

Python projects: guess a number that is randomly selected, n.d.

In the next game, I limit the number of chances a user can have while guessing the number. A player has eight chances to guess the number. When the game ends, you will be asked to play again or exit the game. Here is the code for the game.

```
of random import randint
name = input ("Welcome! First enter your name:")
print (name + "I welcome you to the number game")
def game ():
rand_number = randint (0,100) # Generates a random number
print ("\ nFor this game I selected a random number between 1 and 100 ...")
print ("Be accurate and smart. You only have 8 chances to guess the number ...")
i = 1
r = 1
while I <9: # you have 8 chances
user_number = int (input ('Enter any number you want:'))
as user number <edge number:
print ("\ n" + name + ", the correct number is higher than the number you guessed")
print ("Now you have" + str (8-i) + "chances left")
i = i + 1
```

```
elif user_number> rand_number:
print ("\ n" + name + ", the correct number is lower than the
number you guessed")
print ("you have now" + str (8-i) + "chances left")
i = i + 1
elif user_number == rand_number:
print ("\ nMany congratulations" + name + "!! You guessed the
right number!")
r = 0;
break
different:
print ("You have entered an invalid number. Please try again")
print ("Now you have" + str (8-i) + "chances left")
continue
if r == 1:
print ("Sorry you couldn't win the game !!")
print ("The correct number is =" + str (rand_number))
def main ():
game()
while true:
another_game = input ("Do you want to play another game? (y /
n):")
if another_game == "y":
game()
different:
break
head ()
print ("\ nThis is the end of the game! Thank you very much for
playing. Come back another time!")
============== RESTART: C: \ Users \ saifia computers \
Desktop \ Python.py =============
Welcome! First enter your name: John
John, I welcome you to the numbers game
```

For this game I selected a random number between 1 and 100 ...
Be accurate and smart. You only have 8 chances to guess the
number ...
Enter any number: 30
John, the correct number is higher than the one you guessed
Now you have 7 chances left
Enter any number: 40
John, the correct number is higher than the one you guessed
Now you have 6 chances left
Enter any number: 50
John, the correct number is less than the number you guessed
you now have 5 chances left
Enter any number: 49
John, the correct number is less than the number you guessed
you have now left 4 chances
Enter any number: 48
John, the correct number is less than the number you guessed
you have now left 3 chances
Enter any number: 47
John, the correct number is less than the number you guessed
you have now left 2 chances
Enter any number: 46
John, the correct number is less than the number you guessed
you have now left 1 chance
Enter any number: 45
Congratulations, John !! You have successfully guessed the
correct number!
Do you want to play another game? (y / n): n
This is the end of the game! Thank you very much for playing.
Come back another time!
>>>

The game at the beginning asks you to enter your name. When you enter it, you can continue playing the game. I had exhausted my chances, but managed to guess the right number on the last attempt. You can change the code and maximize or minimize the number of attempts it takes to guess the correct number. You can also change the range of words. For example, you can start from one and end at 1000 to make it a bit more challenging, but you will have to increase the number of opportunities. Otherwise, players may quickly get bored with the game.

Python projects: guess a number that is randomly selected, n.d.

Rock Paper Scissor Game
This is another python program that allows users to play the rock paper and scissor game. I made the code that you can copy and paste in the editor and play the game in the shell.
# I will import random module just like I did to guess the numbers game
import randomly
# You must print multi-line instructions
# It is better to do string concatenation of all strings in print statement print ("Here I will define the winning rules for Rock paper scissor game. They are as under: \ n"
+ "Rock vs paper-> paper won the game \ n"
+ "Rock vs scissors-> Rock has won \ n"
+ "paper vs scissor-> scissor has won \ n")

while true:
print ("Please enter your choice \ n 1. Rock \ n 2. paper \ n 3. scissors \ n")

```python
# This function takes the input from the user. We have fully
defined the input function
choice = int (input ("This is the user's turn:"))


# OR is definitely a short circuit operator
# if only a single condition is true
# It returns a True value

# The code performs a loop function until the user enters an
invalid entry
while choice> 3 or choice <1:
choice = int (input ("You must enter a valid input:"))



# You must initialize a value for the variable choice_name
as choice == 1:
choice_names = 'Rock'
elif choice == 2:
choice_names = 'paper'
different:
choice_names = 'scissors'

# You must print the user's choice
print ("User's choice is:" + choice_names)
print ("\ nYou are done. Now it is your turn to turn .......")

# The computer dials a random number
# between 1, 2 and 3. You must use the randint method
# this is from the random module
comp_choice = random.randint (1, 3)

# The program will run loops up to the comp_choice value
# equals choice value
```

```python
while comp_choice == choice:
comp_choice = random.randint (1, 3)

# You must initialize the value of comp_choice_name
if comp_choice == 1:
comp_choice_names = 'Rock'
elif comp_choice == 2:
comp_choice_names = 'paper'
different:
comp_choice_names = 'scissors'

print ("The choice of the computer is:" + comp_choice_names)

print (choice_names + "V / s" + comp_choice_names)

if ((choice == 1 and comp_choice == 2) or
(choice == 2 and comp_choice == 1)):
print ("paper wins the game =>", end = "")
result = "paper"

elif ((choice == 1 and comp_choice == 3) or
(choice == 3 and comp_choice == 1)):
print ("Rock wins the game =>", end = "")
result = "Rock"
different:
print ("scissors win the game =>", end = "")
result = "scissor"

as a result == choice_names:
print ("<The player has won>")
different:
print ("<Computer has won>")
```

```python
print ("Have fun! Wonder if you want to play again? (Y / N)")
ans = input ()

if ans == 'n' or ans == 'N':
break


# after coming out of the while loop
# we print thanks for playing
print ("\ nThanks for playing the game")
```
============= RESTART: C: \ Users \ saifia computers \ Desktop \ Python.py =============
Here I will determine the winning rules for Rock Paper Scissor game. They are as under:
Rock vs paper-> paper won the game
Rock vs scissor-> Rock has won
paper vs scissor-> scissor has won
You must enter your choice
1. Rock
2. paper
3. scissors
This is the user's turn: 2
The choice of the user is: paper
You're done. Now it is the turn of the computer ....
The choice of the computer is: scissors
paper V / s scissors
scissors win the game => <computer won>
I had fun! I wonder if you want to play again? (Y / N)
y
You must enter your choice
1. Rock
2. paper
3. scissors
This is the user's turn: 1

The user's choice is: Rock
You're done. Now it is the turn of the computer ....
The choice of the computer is: scissors
Rock V / s scissors
Rock wins the game => <The player has won>
I had fun! I wonder if you want to play again? (Y / N)
y
You must enter your choice
1. Rock
2. paper
3. scissors
This is the user's turn: 3
The user's choice is: scissors
You're done. Now it is the turn of the computer ....
The choice of the computer is: paper
scissors V / s paper
scissors win the game => <The player has won>
I had fun! I wonder if you want to play again? (Y / N)
n
Thanks for playing the game
>>>
(Python | Program to implement Rock paper scissor game, n.d)

Python calculator

The following program is for creating a simple four function calculator.

```
# This program helps you to create a simple calculator
# The following function adds two numbers
def addition (y, z):
return y + z
# The following function subtracts the two numbers
```

```python
subtract def (y, z):
return y - z
# The following function multiplies the two numbers
def multiplication (y, z):
return y * z
# The following function divides the two numbers
def division (y, z):
return y / z
print ("You must select the operation.")
print ("1.Add the numbers")
print ("2. Subtract the numbers")
print ("3.Multiple numbers")
print ("4.Divide the numbers")
# You must copy the user's input
choice = input ("You must enter the choice (1/2/3/4):")
number1 = float (input ("Enter the first number:"))
number2 = float (input ("Enter the second number:"))
as choice == '1':
print (number1, "+", number2, "=", addition (number1,
number2))
elif choice == '2':
print (number1, "-", number2, "=", subtract (number1,
number2))
elif choice == '3':
print (number1, "*", number2, "=", multiplication (number1,
number2))
elif choice == '4':
print (number1, "/", number2, "=", division (number1,
number2))
different:
print ("The input is invalid")
============== RESTART: C: \ Users \ saifia computers \
Desktop \ Python.py =============
```

You must select the operation.
1. add the numbers
2. Subtract the numbers
Multiply the numbers
4. Divide the numbers
You must enter the choice (1/2/3/4): 1
Enter the first number: 100
Enter the second number: 50
100.0 + 50.0 = 150.0
>>>
============== RESTART: C: \ Users \ saifia computers \ Desktop \ Python.py ==============
You must select the operation.
1. add the numbers
2. Subtract the numbers
Multiply the numbers
4. Divide the numbers
You must enter the choice (1/2/3/4): 2
Enter the first number: 100
Enter the second number: 50
100.0 - 50.0 = 50.0
>>>
============== RESTART: C: \ Users \ saifia computers \ Desktop \ Python.py ==============
You must select the operation.
1. add the numbers
2. Subtract the numbers
Multiply the numbers
4. Divide the numbers
You must enter the choice (1/2/3/4): 3
Enter the first number: 50
Enter the second number: 2
50.0 * 2.0 = 100.0

```
>>>
============= RESTART: C: \ Users \ saifia computers \
Desktop \ Python.py =============
>>>
You must select the operation.
1. Add the numbers
2. Subtract the numbers
Multiply the numbers
4. Divide the numbers
You must enter the selection (1/2/3/4): 4
Enter the first number: 500
Enter the second number: 100
500.0 / 100.0 = 5.0
>>>
```

(Python program to make a simple calculator, nd)

Python password generator

From cleaning services to financial consultancies, everyone needs a strong password. Cyber security is becoming more important every day as hackers are always trying to penetrate computer systems and mobile phones. Therefore, you need a powerful password generator that will save you time and money by generating passwords for you. This is the best way forward. The following program generates passwords for you.

```
import randomly
def genPword (pwlength):
alph = "abcdefghijklmnopqrstuvwxyz"
pwords = []
for i in pwlength:

pword = ""
```

```python
for j in range (i):
next_letter_index = random.randrange (len (alf))
pword = pword + alph [next_letter_index]


pword = ReplaceWithNumber (pword)
pword = ReplaceWithUppercaseLetter (pword)


pwords.append (pword)


return pwords
def ReplaceWithNumber (password):
for i within range (random.randrange (1,3)):
Replace_index = random.randrange (len (password) // 2)
password = password [0: replace_index] + str
(random.randrange (10)) + password [replace_index + 1:]
return password
def replaWithUppercaseLetter (password):
for i within range (random.randrange (1,3)):
Replace_index = random.randrange (len (password) // 2, len
(password))
password = password [0: replace_index] + password
[replace_index] .upper () + password [replace_index + 1:]
return password
def main ():
numPwords = int (input ("Can you specify how many passwords
to generate?"))


print ("The program generates" + str (numPwords) +
"passwords for you")


pwordLengths = []
print ("The lowest number of passwords must be three")
for i within range (numPwords):
```

```
length = int (input ("You must enter the length of Password #" +
str (i + 1) + ""))
if length <3:
length = 3
pwordLengths.append (length)


Pword = genPword (pwordLengths)
for i within range (numPwords):
print ("Password #" + str (i + 1) + "=" + Pword [i])
head ()
============= RESTART: C: \ Users \ saifia computers \
Desktop \ Python.py =============
Can you indicate how many passwords you need to generate? 5
The program generates 5 passwords for you
The lowest number of passwords should be three
You must enter the length of password 1 12
You must enter the length of password # 2 13
You must enter the length of password # 3 15
You must enter the length of password # 4 20
You must enter the length of password # 5 45
Password # 1 = tf1yaoXtbfxv
Password # 2 = emf7txnxHgxuu
Password # 3 = pocfq7vyxqlFzcr
Password # 4 = ppuhv7lagsvockgvoRyg
Password # 5 =
nbpccfvcqqmmyieovhc3prburpkenufvakpyzkhawujeC
>>>
Roll the dice
# First of all, you need to import the module to generate random
numbers
import randomly
#Here you have to decide on the range of values of your dice
min_value = 1
```

```
max_value = 10
#Here you have to go through this through the user input
roll_again = "yes"
#time to make a loop
while roll_again == "yes" or roll_again == "y":
print ("I roll the dice ...")
print ("Show us the values:")


#this will generate or print the first random integer from 1 to 6
print (random.randint (min_value, max_value))


#this generates or prints the 2nd random integer from 1 to 6
print (random.randint (min_value, max_value))


#This will ask the player to roll the dice again. Any input other
than yes or y will definitely end the loop
roll_again = input ("Do you want to roll the dice again?")
============== RESTART: C: \ Users \ saifia computers \
Desktop \ Python.py =============
I roll the dice ...
Let's take a look at the values:
10
3
Do you want to roll the dice again? y
I roll the dice ...
Let's take a look at the values:
1
9
Do you want to roll the dice again? y
I roll the dice ...
Let's take a look at the values:
10
10
```

Do you want to roll the dice again? y
I roll the dice ...
Let's take a look at the values:
7
3
Do you want to roll the dice again? y
I roll the dice ...
Let's take a look at the values:
10
1
Do you want to roll the dice again? n
>>>

Executioner

This is another Python game to guess the correct word.

```
import randomly
import sys
# It's time to set a few variables
wordList = [
"zebra", "window", "cushion", "glass", "dressing table", "table",
"quilt",
"laptop", "bed", "vulture", "cat", "sewing machine", "cable",
"powder", "TV"]
guess_word = []
secWord = random.choice (wordList)
len_word = len (secWord)
alph = "abcdefghijklmnopqrstuvwxyz"
letter_storage = []
def start ():
print ("Hello player! \ n")
while true:
```

```python
name = input ("You can enter your name \ n"). strip ()
as name == ":
print ("You don't have permission to do that! Can't leave blank
lines")
different:
break
get started()
def newFunc ():
print ("Well, let's play Hangman! \ n")
while true:
gameChoice = input ("Are you ready to play? \ n"). upper ()
if gameChoice == "YES" or gameChoice == "Y":
break
elif gameChoice == "NO" or gameChoice == "N":
sys.exit ("I'm disappointed! Good day")
different:
print ("You only have to answer with a Yes or No")
continue
newFunc ()
def change ():
for character in secWord:
guess_word.append ("-")
print ("Your guessed word has" len_word "," characters ")
print ("You only have the option to enter only 1 letter, starting
with a-z \ n \ n")
print (guess_word)
def guess ():
guess_taken = 1
while guess_ taken <15:
guess = input ("You must choose one letter \ n"). lower ()
if not guess in alpha: # let's start checking the input
print ("You must enter one letter from a-z alphabet")
guess elif in letter_storage:
```

```
print ("Dear, you guessed it!")
different:
letter_storage.append (recommend)
as guess in secWord:
print ("You've guessed the right word successfully!")
for x in range (0, len_word):
if secWord [x] == guess:
guess_word [x] = guess
print (guess_word)
if not '-' in guess_word:
print ("Congratulations! You won the game!")
break
different:
print ("Failed! The letter cannot be traced in the word. You must
try again!")
guess_tasks + = 1
if guess_ = 10 =:
print ("Sorry honey, you lost the game: <! My secret word is",
secWord)
change()
guess ()
print ("Game Over!")
=========== RESTART: C: \ Users \ saifia computers \ Desktop
\ Python.py ==========
Hello player!
You can enter your name
John Wick
Well, let's play Hangman!
Are you ready to play?
Yes
Your guessed word has 2 characters
You only have the option to enter only 1 letter starting with a-z
['-', '-']
```

You must choose one letter

a

Failure! The letter cannot be traced in the word. You must try again!

You must choose one letter

b

Failure! The letter cannot be traced in the word. You must try again!

You must choose one letter

c

Failure! The letter cannot be traced in the word. You must try again!

You must choose one letter

d

Failure! The letter cannot be traced in the word. You must try again!

You must choose one letter

e

Failure! The letter cannot be traced in the word. You must try again!

You must choose one letter

f

Failure! The letter cannot be traced in the word. You must try again!

You must choose one letter

g

Failure! The letter cannot be traced in the word. You must try again!

You must choose one letter

h

Failure! The letter cannot be traced in the word. You must try again!

You must choose one letter

I

Failure! The letter cannot be traced in the word. You must try again!

Sorry honey you lost the game: My secret word is TV

You must choose one letter

=========== RESTART: C: \ Users \ saifia computers \ Desktop \ Python.py ==========

Hello player!

You can enter your name

John Wick

Well, let's play Hangman!

Are you ready to play?

Yes

Your guessed word has 14 characters

You only have the option to enter only 1 letter starting with a-z

["-", "-", "-", "-", "-", "-", "-", "-", "-", "-", "-", "-", " - ',' - ']

You must choose one letter

d

You have successfully guessed the right word!

['d', '-', '-', '-', '-', '-', '-', '-', '-', '-', '-', '-', ' - ',' - ']

You must choose one letter

e

You have successfully guessed the right word!

['d', '-', 'e', '-', '-', '-', '-', '-', '-', '-', '-', '-', '-', '-']

['d', '-', 'e', '-', '-', '-', '-', '-', '-', '-', '-', '-', ' - ',' e ']

You must choose one letter

f

Failure! The letter cannot be traced in the word. You must try again!

You must choose one letter

g

You have successfully guessed the right word!

['d', '-', 'e', '-', '-', '-', '-', 'g', '-', '-', '-', '-', ' - ',' e ']

You must choose one letter

h

Failure! The letter cannot be traced in the word. You must try again!

You must choose one letter

I

You have successfully guessed the right word!

['d', '-', 'e', '-', '-', 'i', '-', 'g', '-', '-', '-', '-', ' - ',' e ']

You must choose one letter

j

Failure! The letter cannot be traced in the word. You must try again!

You must choose one letter

k

Failure! The letter cannot be traced in the word. You must try again!

You must choose one letter

l

You have successfully guessed the right word!

['d', '-', 'e', '-', '-', 'i', '-', 'g', '-', '-', '-', '-', 'l', 'e']

You must choose one letter

m

Failure! The letter cannot be traced in the word. You must try again!

You must choose one letter

n

You have successfully guessed the right word!

['d', '-', 'e', '-', '-', 'i', 'n', 'g', '-', '-', '-', '-', 'l', 'e']

You must choose one letter

o

Failure! The letter cannot be traced in the word. You must try again!

You must choose one letter

p
Failure! The letter cannot be traced in the word. You must try again!
You must choose one letter
q
Failure! The letter cannot be traced in the word. You must try again!
You must choose one letter
r
You have successfully guessed the right word!
['d', 'r', 'e', '-', '-', 'i', 'n', 'g', '-', '-', '-', '-' , 'l', 'e']
You must choose one letter
s
You have successfully guessed the right word!
['d', 'r', 'e', 's', '-', 'i', 'n', 'g', '-', '-', '-', '-' , 'l', 'e']
['dressing', '-', '-', '-', '-', 'l', 'e']
You must choose one letter
t
You have successfully guessed the right word!
['d', 'r', 'e', 's', 's', 'i', 'n', 'g', '-', 't', '-', '-' , 'l', 'e']
You must choose one letter
you
Failure! The letter cannot be traced in the word. You must try again!
Sorry honey you lost the game: My secret word is dressing table
You must choose one letter
v
Failure! The letter cannot be traced in the word. You must try again!
You must choose one letter
w
Failure! The letter cannot be traced in the word. You must try again!

You must choose one letter
X
Failure! The letter cannot be traced in the word. You must try
again!
You must choose one letter
y
Failure! The letter cannot be traced in the word. You must try
again!
You must choose one letter
z
Failure! The letter cannot be traced in the word. You must try
again!
Game is over!
>>>
(Another Python Hangman, n.d)

I made two attempts, but it failed. You now know the technique
to both develop the game and play the game. You can fill in the
game with different letters to guess the word just like me. The
game is developed in the text editor but played in the shell. You
can add graphical interfaces to make the game usable for your
kids. You need to read all the codes given in these Python
projects. You can change them at will as you can now easily
understand the script.

They all contain functions, lists, dictionaries, before and while
loops and printing instructions. You have already read, practiced
and seen how they were used in different Python programs. You
need to understand the Python projects script and then form it
according to your custom requirements and then develop a new
project based on this code. This is how you can build a python
program from scratch.

Inference

Python has many advantages for programmers. It is a language remarkable for the ease of learning. It can be used as a stepping stone to learning other complex languages and different systems such as artificial intelligence and machine learning. If you are an absolute beginner, this is what you definitely enjoy and long for learning other languages.

Python is one of the most widely used languages in the world. Google, Disney, Nokia, IBM, Instagram are some examples of companies that use Python for daily activities. They rely on Python to perform their services. Raspberry Pi, similar to a mini computer, is based on Python as the main programming language. If you know Python, you can easily be a master of Raspberry Pi. Once you have mastered the art of Python, you can use it in many ways, such as in web applications, mobile applications and AI systems. Today, companies are moving toward different business strategies based on machine learning and AI to increase their revenues. An example is an efficient chatbot that saves companies time and money. There are several companies that rely on Python; therefore you can make very good money if you learn programming in Python.

Python is always behind on the different prototypes. Python provides users with a productive coding environment that would lead to more skills learning. The best thing about Python is that it is very easy to read. You have read the codes I have written for you. They are fun to read and easy to understand and internalize. That is why Python should be at the top of the languages you need to learn.

www.ingramcontent.com/pod-product-compliance
Lightning Source LLC
Chambersburg PA
CBHW071426150726
48000CB00001B/493